HET BUN DAI BUN

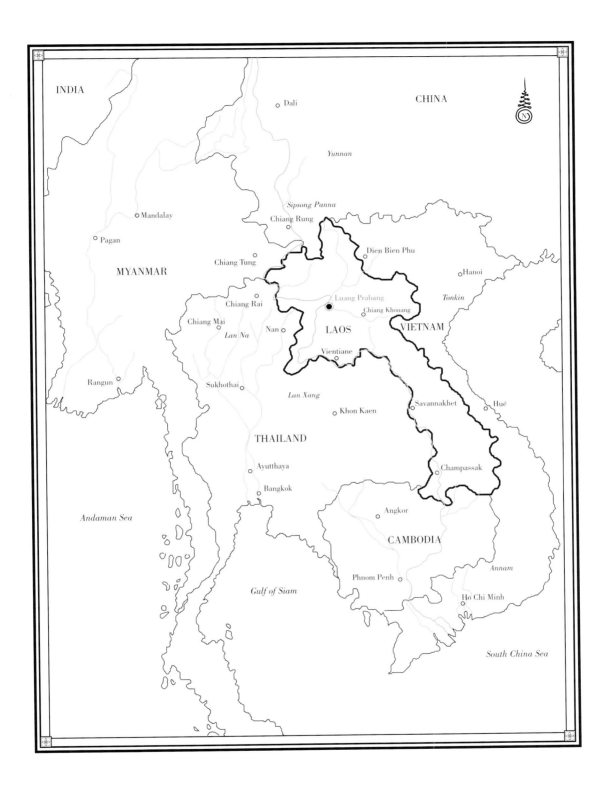

First published in Great Britain in 2000
by Westzone Publishing Ltd
19 Clifford Street, London W1X 1RH, UK

© Hans Georg Berger 2000

10 9 8 7 6 5 4 3 2 1

A catalogue record for this book is
available from the British Library

ISBN: 0 903391 02 4

Edited and produced by Gigi Giannuzzi

Maps by Tawatchai Kulthavarakorn

Translations by Ann Robertson (texts by Hans Georg Berger
and Wibke Lobo) and Martin Barr (text by Christian Caujolle)

Design by Manuel Orio and Salomé Nascimento

Cover design by Rose Design Associates, London

Original silver prints on barytic paper printed by Atélier
Fenêtre sur Cour, Paris, France, under the supervision
of the photographer.

Hans Georg Berger's work in Luang Prabang was subsidised
by a grant from the Ministry of Foreign Affairs of the Federal
Republic of Germany and organised in collaboration with the
Ministry of Information and Culture of the Lao People's
Democratic Republic

Colour separation and print in Belgium by Salto

HET BUN DAI BUN

LAOS – SACRED RITUALS OF LUANG PRABANG

HANS GEORG BERGER

westzone

with texts by:
Christian Caujolle
Volker Grabowsky
Wibke Lobo
Pha One Keo Sitthivong

Christian Caujolle

A Sympathetic Glance
Remarks on a body of photographs by Hans Georg Berger

If I can be forgiven the analogy – which will seem out of place in the context of these Buddhist lands – anyone fortunate enough to have visited and stayed in Luang Prabang will have experienced something akin to what Catholics commonly refer to as Paradise. If Paradise exists anywhere on earth, it may well be found on the banks of the Mekong, where understated beauty combines with the abiding charm derived from meeting the gentle monks and visiting the ever beautiful temples with their open courtyards, which always hold their share of surprise. One must witness, at dusk, the groups of orange-robed novices with their black umbrellas, follow the road that skirts the Mekong *en route* to pray with the eldest monks, to understand the extent to which – in a completely natural way – this particular culture's aesthetics, discipline, philosophy, relations with others and religion all combine to enable man, who is not wise at all, to become that little bit wiser.

These sentiments, based on my regrettably brief visits to Luang Prabang, are rekindled as I look through the photographs that Hans Georg Berger brought back from his many and prolonged stays in Luang Prabang. In his square-shaped images, which document both temple life and key moments of religious festivals relating to the seasons, the elements, the ever-present water and moments of prayer, I rediscover the overwhelming sense of peace that I experienced upon arrival in this city. The deportment of the locals – the slow gestures, the distinctive way they carry themselves and the display of mutual respect shown for each other – personify peace and contentment.

What strikes me as significant is that this long work of visual investigation was carried out at the very time when, in Laos, Buddhism is enjoying an exemplary revival. During this revival, hundreds of young people learn from their elders, who have preserved intact the memory and practice of a religion oblivious to masochism, the essence of an altruistic philosophy. From this perspective, Hans Georg Berger's work constitutes an irreplaceable document.
The work's greatest value, however, derives from the fact that, by being accessible to Laotian schoolchildren in a schoolbook format, it will enable those children to acquaint themselves with their country's culture and tradition after many years during which the teaching of those subjects had been banned. In my view, this surpasses even the quality of the work.

The square format of the photographs adds to the impression of poise that one gets from surveying this work. The work records in black and white the variations of light on both subjects and locations. It is, at first glance, documentary in nature, giving shape to and recording the activities that occur during the year, and enhancing our knowledge in the process. In this approach to photography, which has yielded a unique corpus, there is a marked humility that has its origins in both the locations and the subjects of the photographs. This *oeuvre* reminds us of two things. Firstly that if you want to achieve quality in photography, you have to consider time as a partner. Secondly, it brings to mind the current developments in a genre of photography, scorned for a long time, that has been called, rather condescendingly, 'ethnographic photography'. It is remarkable to note the extent to which, by refusing to restrict themselves exclusively to a descriptive point of view – even while continuing to be documentary – a small number of authors, in the last five years, has revived this genre. In the 1930s and at the time of the great ethnological missions, the practice of photography consisted mainly in creating records to be taken back as testimony and as objects to be studied (compare the plundering of statues or ritual objects). This contrasts with a 'new' ethnographic photography, which has chosen a different set of objectives. This kind of photography is respectful, seeking both to describe and to understand. To this end, it eschews, *vis-à-vis* its subject, an outside stance so as to convey not so much the subject's difference or otherness but, rather, its internal coherence, logic and lines of force. Such a project implies a rigour of form, which can sometimes be repetitive, and an absence of spectacular views. The choice of the square format supports such a calm and respectful approach, and sets down precise choices of the distances from which the photographer views his subject. The photographer, though an outsider, tries to blend in with the community as much as possible in order not to disturb the unfolding of events to which he has been granted access. The optimal distance will be that from which the photographer can reproduce the unfolding events without exaggerating them, which he will occasionally translate into sequences or series. The choice of black and white not only avoids the pitfalls of glossy exoticism, but also evokes an ambience that makes us aware of the all-pervading harmony in which everything is bathed. In these images, we follow the profoundly rich traditions that the inhabitants and monks of the old capital of the 'kingdom of a million elephants and the white umbrella' have preserved: from the ordination of monks to funerary rites; from the rowing festival to the rites of newborn babies.

In this collective memoir, formed over five years of campaigning shots, we must look separately at two discrete sets of images. First, there are the documentary images relating to the architecture, objects of ritual and manuscripts written on palm leaves. These constitute a remarkable set of images which, together with the current restoration work taking place in the city, will protect a priceless cultural heritage against disappearing.

Second, there is the set of images, perhaps the richest part of the *oeuvre*, which consist of posed portraits – of individuals and groups alike – often taken during key moments of religious life. In these calm one-to-ones, a rare thing in portraiture, there is a surprising relationship of equality between the individuals on either side of the camera, which makes it difficult to use the formulaic phrase, to 'take' a photograph. Rather, one has the impression that, between the photographer and his subjects, the usual situation of confrontation is substituted by an exchange where the people on both sides of the camera freely give to each other whatever they have.

One remarkable achievement of Berger's work on the sacred rituals of Luang Prabang is to remind us that these traditions, long preserved by memory before being captured by photography, are above all founded on the principle of mutual respect.

Christian Caujolle is director of the Vu photographers' agency and of the gallery of the same name in Paris.

Wibke Lobo

The Middle Way

Theravada Buddhism and its special nature in Laos

'This is my final birth', thunders the lion-like voice of Siddhartha in all directions of the compass as he emerges into the world from the right hip of his mother, Maya, and takes his first seven steps. As fruits of his good deeds in previous existences, he bears on his body the thirty-two signs of a Great Man which destine him to become either a world-ruling king or a Buddha. Siddhartha grows up well-protected in the palace of his father, a landed noble, and he enjoys all the pleasures of a luxurious, sensuous existence. Nevertheless, at the age of twenty-nine he decides to give up his seemingly carefree life. During three outings he sees an old man, a sick man and a dead man, and he recognises that all beings are inevitably subject to this fearful destiny. On a fourth excursion he sees a wandering ascetic and interprets this as the sign of the way that he himself must take in order to discover the deep truths of existence. He secretly leaves his wife and newborn child by night and moves 'from home into homelessness'. He discards the tokens of his elevated status, his magnificent robes, his jewellery, his turban; he cuts off his hair with his sword and becomes a wandering ascetic in search of enlightenment. He learns from wise yoga masters, subjects himself to the most severe self-discipline, but he still does not find the liberating answers to his questions. Finally, almost starved to a skeleton, he decides to abandon his rigorous exercises and depart on a moderate 'Middle Way'. He goes to bathe in a river; he accepts nourishment again; he sits beneath a fig tree, and finally he starts to meditate. At first he is disturbed by Mara, the personification of the eternal cycle of life and death, which he would like to overcome. He manages to gain power over him through the strength of his concentration and then gradually progresses into the four stages of contemplation which lead him to enlightenment. His lucid mind recognises three basic conditions: he sees that all beings involved in the turmoil of the cycle of birth are reborn into better or worse existences as a result of their good or bad deeds. He remembers all his earlier existences, and finally he identifies the Four Noble Truths of Suffering: he recognises what constitutes suffering (the transience of all life), the cause of suffering (the desire for life which leads to ever new existences), the way to overcome suffering (breaking the chain of cause and effect), and the way to stop desiring and suffering (the Noble Eightfold Path). At this point he entered into buddhahood. He had become a Buddha, an 'Awakened, Enlightened One' and had attained a state of absolute peace and spiritual bliss, nirvana. His outstanding virtues are omniscience and great compassion. As he has perceived that there is no eternal, unalterable self, no individual soul that remains after life has left the body, he is certain that, as he announced at his birth, he will never be born again. The omen of his name Siddhartha, 'he who has attained his goal', has reached fulfilment. Near Benares, in the Gazelle Grove of Sarnath, he speaks for the very first time about his insights to just five listeners. In this sermon he imparts the 'Four Noble Truths of Suffering', and explains that it is not life itself that is full of suffering, but the fact of its transience. At this point he 'sets the Wheel of Law into motion'. From now on, he will wander the lands until his eightieth birthday, he will gather a great number of followers around him and, in his great compassion for those trapped in ignorance and buffeted from one existence to the next, he will teach about enlightenment. His death is mourned painfully by all who are close to him, but the gods celebrate this event with music and showers of blossoms, because the Buddha has now entered for ever into the 'Great Complete Nirvana' (*mahaparinirvana*) as a result of all his merits and his spiritual lucidity.

Siddhartha Gautama was a member of the Shakyas and also known as Shakyamuni which means the Wise One of the House of Shakya. He was active in northern India around 500 BC and is the ideal and inspiration of all Buddhists. In Laos, as in other countries where Theravada Buddhism is prevalent, both he and the legends from his life have a fundamental significance. Having departed to the complete nirvana the Buddha will no longer actively intervene in human existence. Yet his unmistakable image is a source of spiritual strength to his followers, and his life story sets their moral standards. In most pagodas, wall paintings illustrate the legendary and historical episodes of his life, as they contain the key thoughts of his message and can be easily understood by all. The monks follow in Buddha's footsteps and study his teachings with great dedication. The three pillars, also known as 'The Triple Jewel': the Buddha, the Law (*dharma*) and the Monastic Community (*sangha*), form the core of the Theravada tradition which refers back to the teachings of the elders who either knew the Buddha personally or were taught by his senior monks (Theravada: 'Words of the Elders').

The teachings of the Buddha represent a path towards self-enlightenment. In his day this was a revolutionary philosophy which professed that the way of life and intellectual strength are the decisive factors in the approach to enlightenment, as opposed to hereditary status, i.e. the caste. His teachings make great demands on the individual's morality and intellect. Freedom from the constraints of time is essential when following the Noble Eightfold Path with its eight elements: right views, right intention, right speech, right action, right livelihood, right effort, right awareness, and right concentration. Thus the monks and nuns, who do not have to support their own material existence, have the best chance of attaining enlightenment as they can devote their entire energy to spiritual perfection. Here, the emphasis lies in personal effort. As the Buddha showed through his own life, the means of achieving wise insight is meditation. It is a method of controlling thoughts so that the good energies of the intellect can develop and then determine the action, rather than the evil energies. When the spirit has been cleansed of the four basic evils of greed, hatred, delusion and ignorance, then wisdom and goodness are free to develop, and the way is open to achieve a state of joy and ease, and eventually a state of pure peace, that is nirvana. In Laos, nirvana is popularly seen as a place of perfect joy where all desires have been fulfilled. Most people believe that they will attain enlightenment at the end of the present age of the world when Maitreya, the future Buddha and saviour, appears. But until then they will live through many existences, striving to gain merits by doing good deeds and avoiding bad ones. As every good deed erases a bad one, they are able to cleanse themselves of their sins and so work towards making the present and future existence happier.

The desire to gain merits is a decisive factor in the lives of the Buddhist Lao people. They can do this as lay people not only by following the five rules of moral conduct (do not kill, do not steal, do not live in sexual excess, do not lie and do not abuse intoxicating substances), but especially through generosity. Supporting the monastic community earns greater merit than any other good deed. But a donation to an abbot is far weightier than a donation to a freshly ordained monk or particularly a novice. This is where the women especially can do good deeds to improve their karma, for it is usually the women who fill the monks' rice bowls on their daily round for alms. It is also the women's task to prepare the food and floral decorations for the ceremonies to make them dignified and aesthetically pleasing events. A fundamental aspect of Buddhism in Laos is the concept of transferring merits. Anybody, whether a monk or a lay person, can give their merits away, especially to the dead. In the same way as they are grateful to their ancestors for giving them life, they in turn can contribute to the improvement of the deceased's karma. The act of transferring merits not only helps avoid the dangers of selfishness which can lie hidden in the conception of self-enlightenment, it also strengthens the sense of responsibility towards the community. In the final instance, unselfishness is the virtue which determines the quality of a person's deeds.

Within the present area of Laos, Theravada Buddhism began spreading in the twelfth century and was established as the state religion around 1350 when the kingdom of Laos was founded. A symbiotic relationship developed between Theravada Buddhism and ancient, deep-rooted local rites, especially animism. Characteristic features of this include the belief in the *khuan*, certain powers which dwell in every being or object. These powers are treated as living beings and the Lao people honour them at the *su-khuan* celebrations on all important occasions, such as birth, marriage, the initiation of novices, or the festival in thanks for a bountiful harvest. Although the monks do not participate in this ceremony, they accept it as an integral part of the Buddhist way of life. And it is equally natural that the *phi*, the local protective spirits, are integrated into the Buddhist system. The little houses, which the people build for them and regularly supply with offerings, can be found not only on the land of the lay people but also in the grounds of pagodas and monasteries. Brahmanic concepts, which already existed before the spread of Buddhism, have also survived in various rites. The holy white cord which the monks wind round the statue of the Buddha during the ceremony of transferring merits to the dead, and the pouring of consecrated water onto the earth, are both of Brahmanic origin. The veneration of the snake-like *naga*, which dwell in the rivers and represent the power of water as the bearer of fertility, is known to have existed in pre-Buddhist times and has been preserved in Laos particularly in connection with the festival of boats.

As the state religion, Theravada Buddhism enjoyed the protection of the king, but it still had to recognise his sovereignty. The identification of the ruler with the religion crystalised in the concept of the Buddha as king, as expressed in the statue of Pra Bang. This particular Buddha figure is royally adorned and dressed in a sumptuous robe. It was the palladium, the ultimate source of protection for the kingdom of Laos, and this statue still stands in the former royal palace, now the National Museum, in Luang Prabang. After the socialist revolution of the Pathet Lao in 1975, this particular aspect of the banned religion was especially taboo. But today, in a ceremony led by state officials and accompanied by monks, the Pra Bang is again carried through Luang Prabang during the New Year celebrations which were traditionally closely associated with the legitimisation of the monarch's power. The fact that the Lao government recently commissioned the construction of an impressive, magnificently decorated pagoda for the statue in the park of the National Museum clearly shows that the belief in the magic power of the Pra Bang is still very much alive.

Bibliography:
H. Bechert and R. Gombrich, *The World of Buddhism* (London: Thames and Hudson, 1984)
M. Zago, *Rites et cérémonies en milieu bouddhiste Lao.* (Roma: Università Gregoriana Editrice, 1972).

Wibke Lobo, Dr phil., is head of the department of South and Southeast Asia at the Ethnologisches Museum, Staatliche Museen zu Berlin, Stiftung Preussischer Kulturbesitz.

One morning, the Enlightened One,
our Lord and Teacher,
looked down from the best of worlds onto the earth.
His gaze fell on Luang Prabang
just as the first ray of sunshine
touched the tip of the mountain Phou-Si.
And a smile appeared on the face of the Enlightened One.

Hans Georg Berger

Het Bun Dai Bun
Art project, meritorious deed, meditative exercise

Within the context of the cultures of Southeast Asia, Laos has developed its own characteristic forms and contents; Lao art has its own distinctive qualities, the literature of Laos, Lao Buddhism, the rituals and ceremonies in Laos, are all different from those of the neighbouring countries. Until now this distinctiveness has hardly been heeded in the West; we know little about the country at the heart of the Southeast Asian peninsula, a country about the size of Great Britain with some five million inhabitants. For decades Laos experienced war, civil war and isolation. Like Vietnam and Cambodia, it was the theatre of colonial conflict which not only lasted for generations and devastated the country's political and social order, but also turned out to be one of the most brutal conflicts of the twentieth century. Despite this, the country has managed to preserve much of the strength of its culture and the core of its civilisation. It sustains its cultural heritage in the rituals of Luang Prabang, a heritage whose beauty instantly touches and speaks to our senses. The photographs and texts in this book tell of these rituals. But they represent only a small selection of the eleven thousand photographs taken during a project that lasted for five years. In the same way, the accompanying texts provide just a brief glimpse through the door that opens into a house full of secrets and surprises. These texts owe a great deal to a key work by Marcello Zago entitled *Rites et cérémonies en milieu bouddhiste lao* and published in 1972. While the work-in-progress was accompanied by the monks themselves, this book proved an invaluable complementary source of advice, and it provided a wealth of background information to what I saw and recorded in the city.

The photographs in this book evolved during a photography project which was conceived and completed together with many people from the city of Luang Prabang. In the early months the monks were the first to take an interest and participate in the project and its aims, but they were soon joined by an increasing number of lay people. We agreed not only to record and document the city's rituals, ceremonies and festivals, thus trying to preserve them for posterity; it was also important to us to support and encourage all those who still continue to celebrate these rituals to this day, as it was clear to us that they would be subject to profound changes in the near future. We agreed that our mutual project would have three stages: first, contemplation of the contents and the approach (which rituals are important to us; where should the camera be placed?); then the photographs themselves (each positioning of the camera was individually discussed); and finally, the assessment and joint selection of the photographs (mounting an exhibition of the photographs in the city's monasteries was part of this project). My authorship of this work is simply a part of this whole. The point of the project was not to fix my personal images of the ceremonies in Luang Prabang in the shape of photographs. On the contrary, my intention was to be involved in the creative, communal production process of a work.

Photography is an artistic medium well suited to comprehending complex cultural relationships and social practices. The constraint of having to continually concentrate on the extract of reality framed by the camera gives rise to very concrete questions about the necessity, the meaning and function of each individual object that will later be visible on the prints. Step by step, the gathering of the pictures leads into the realm of the objects; the eye and the camera are transformed into a teacher who selects the study material. But photography can also promote and organise the participation of many in a mutual, creative project. To put it in western terms, in Luang Prabang we experimented with photography as a process of perception and production, a process that searches for symbolic relationships and which finally culminates in a 'report'. But we also took one further, more decisive step. Through our reflections on the rituals of the city, something new developed in a mutually experienced process – and this could well be the most important aspect of the whole project. It is as if we had been using different layers of tracing paper, each bearing a representation of the same object, and then laid one on top of the other to produce a new, startling image. On the other hand, the people of the city defined and named our project in their own surprising terms. From a Lao point of view we had organised a great *bun* together: a festival, a worthy deed, a great pleasure, a present, something that has a reciprocal effect on all those who participated

in its making. And, as the project progressed, photographing the festivals and ceremonies actually developed into a new ritual for Luang Prabang. It was only logical that the exhibition we presented in nine different monasteries and other sacred places in the city at the end of the project, was opened with a series of diverse ceremonies lasting ten days.

Many of the photographs contained in this book depict people looking into a camera for the first time in their lives. During the project they came closer to and experienced the medium of photography. But photography in general has been present in the life of Luang Prabang for a long time. Although quite isolated from the western world, the royal court of Luang Prabang employed photographers at the beginning of the twentieth century and collected their pictures. As early as the 1920s there were photo studios whose successors now develop the flood of pictures taken by the many tourists who have been flocking into the city since the 1990s. The spiritual elite in the monasteries also looks back on decades of experience with photography. Portraits were taken of eminent abbots from Luang Prabang at least once in their lives. During certain ceremonies (especially the ordination of monks), commemorative photographs were also taken. A number of monks have systematically collected such pictures and preserved them; they were the first people I spoke to when I began my project in 1994. Without their understanding (and their agreement) I would never have been able to carry out my work. They introduced me to the Buddhist perception of pictures, including photographs, which sees in them the reflection of the religious strength and spiritual progress attained by the person portrayed. The wisdom of the portrayed monk radiates back to whoever contemplates such a photograph. In this way the preservation and contemplation of photographs becomes a spiritually healing, meditative exercise. As a result a photograph, like any other sacred image or sculpture, may play a supportive role in every Buddhist's progress along the inner path: therein lies its value. This understanding derives from the *darshan*, the age-old Indian teaching of the power of pictures and visual perception, a classical philosophical system that has remained alive in Buddhism and Hinduism throughout the centuries.

The rites of Luang Prabang create complex relations with the Sacred and generate possibilities of access to salvation for those taking part. This applies equally to Buddhist, Brahmanic and animistic rites. They are always symbolic acts which mean more than is visible at first sight. Their symbolism can only be really understood in the cultural context, in the general view of what constitutes reality, and in the belief of the individual and the group. Each symbol does not simply mean, it *is*: the water at the New Year ritual really does cleanse, yet its purifying qualities mean more than cleansing; the chicken meat that the mother of the newborn baby eats during the *su-khuan* rite is really being shared with the gods Indra and Brahma, to whom the chicken has been dedicated.

Everything that happens during the ritual has to be beautiful and right so that it can be effective; ceremonies that are not beautiful have no effect, no matter how lavish they may be. To the learned Buddhists, the rites and ceremonies of Luang Prabang, which they celebrate with such dignity, are never more than a reflection of what the Enlightened One has taught them to do. They accompany only very indirectly a person's true way to insight and enlightenment. But they are useful because they strengthen religious feeling and help to fulfil the desire for beauty in the world.

Het bun dai bun is the title the people of Luang Prabang gave to our mutual photography project as work progressed. It is a Lao proverb that explains the reward of deeds: whoever does good, the beautiful or the right, will receive the same as a gift in return. The rituals, festivals and ceremonies of Luang Prabang are a contribution to peaceful coexistence and, in the final instance, to the happiness of the city.

A monk dressing

Vat Xiang Muan Vajiramangalarama
26 October 1998, early morning

To Lao Buddhists the monk, who lives according to strict rules in poverty and humility, is the image of the Buddha and the embodiment of the laws he formulated. The monks strive to leave all links with the worldly life behind them in order to attain liberation and salvation. They have given up their family and their work and are entirely dependent on alms from lay people which they collect at dawn during their daily round for alms.

The precepts of the order firmly restrict the monks' personal belongings to eight items. These include their robes, which consist of three pieces of plain material: the undergarment, *antaravasaka;* the outer garment, *uttarasanga*, which is wrapped around the body like a toga and covers one or both of the shoulders, and the *samghati* which is usually just folded and worn over the left shoulder. The robes are orange, saffron or brown, and the material is sewn together in an elaborate, traditionally prescribed way. The lay people give these robes to the monks during their ordination or at the annual *kathin* festival, a deed which earns them special merit.

The personal belongings of a monk:
Three robes
The alms bowl
A belt
An umbrella
A razor
A toothpick

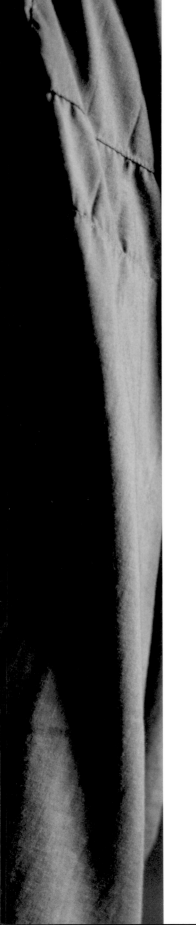

The alms bowl

takbat, the daily round for alms.
The solemn, dignified stance of the monks is an expression
of their first morning meditation on emptiness and the transitory
nature of the gifts they receive.
In front of Vat Xiang Thong Volavihan, at dawn on 22 April 1996

Birth: *su-khuan* ritual for a newborn baby

A house near Vat Aphai
October 1995

The *su-khuan* ritual invokes and celebrates thirty-two spirits of life (the *khuan*) which exist in every human being and protect him or her. This is the most distinctive of all Lao rituals. It accompanies all important changes in life. After the birth of a child it is celebrated for the mother when, after about a month of seclusion, she presents the baby to its father and close relatives for the first time. The ritual expresses honour and respect towards the *khuan*, which are seen as the innermost essence of every life, as the holiest, most powerful and most effective core of every being. The ceremony celebrates the existential circumstances of the human being which consist of the known and the unknown, of fragile reality and attainable reality, of the profane and the sacred.

The *khuan* are neither 'angels' nor 'spirits' that exist independently of a body, nor are they 'souls' possessing spiritual powers. They are the life energies of each and every person that determine the vitality and the equilibrium of all parts of the body, the individual organs and all the abilities of an organism. They have their own life and are different from the body or part of the body in which they reside. Occasionally they can actually leave the body, and this is something they enjoy doing as they are volatile and curious. At such a moment the human being loses his or her equilibrium and becomes sad, weary or ill, until the *su-khuan* ritual reunites the body energies once more. When all the *khuan* depart from a being, it dies. But the *khuan* continue to exist. They will gather together again in a new formation to give their life energies to another being that has just been born.

During the ritual each of the participants ties a cotton thread
around the wrist of the infant, the mother and the father, and later
around the wrists of all the other people present. While doing this,
blessings and good-luck wishes are gently murmured.

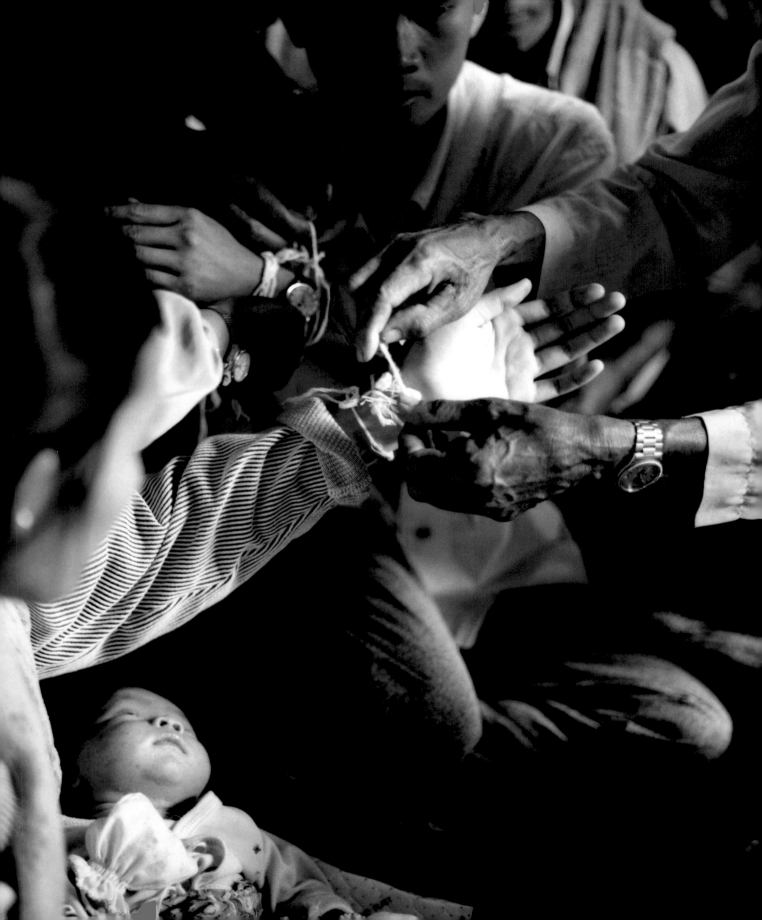

All those present dedicate offerings and the meal for the *khuan*:
flowers or flowering twigs, small candles, cotton threads about
twenty centimetres long; a chicken's egg, rice, small cakes,
bananas, pieces of a cooked chicken and a bottle of rice wine.

The *mo khuan*, who officiates over the ritual, speaks dedication
formulas which strengthen the *khuan* and increase their energies
to make the newborn healthy and, of particular importance, to help
it grow up as a happy child.

The offerings are laid in the mother's hands. She eats from them
and then passes them to the baby's father.
A little alcohol is sprinkled on the floor as a gift to the non-earthly
beings that are invoked during the ritual. Finally, everyone eats
from the offerings. The little cakes, which possess healing powers,
are given to children and the sick.

New Year celebrations

Vat Nong Si Kun Müang
Garden of the former royal palace
Vat Mai
Don Xai Mungkhun, a sandbank on the right bank of the Mekong
April 1996

The Lao year begins with extensive celebrations between the sixth day of the waning moon in the fifth Lao month and the fifth day of the waxing moon in the sixth month. The houses and monasteries of Luang Prabang are cleaned, and water is ritually poured over the city's most important Buddha statues. During the four-day celebrations, processions, pilgrimages to holy grottoes, special presentations of alms for the monks, *su-khuan* ceremonies in the houses, dances and night-time performances gradually develop into high-spirited general festivities. In this period all work should be neglected, otherwise it will bring no luck in the coming year; people wear new clothes and are happy when they get dirty during the celebrations. The ritual pouring of the water, which begins in the monasteries, continues throughout the city during the four days. Water is also sprinkled or poured on monks, dignitaries and older family members as a sign of respect. The more eminent the person, the more often water is poured on them: piety and reverence intermingle with fun and entertainment. In the end, young people drench each other with water, by the bucketful. Here, the initiative is taken especially by the young women and girls. The ritual stands for renewal, cleanliness and fertility, it invokes the rain and creates new life.

Until the revolution in 1975, the king played a special role in many of the New Year celebration rituals. The same applied to numerous other ceremonies in the city: the cult of the country's ancestors, the *naga* cult, and the cult of various local protective holy spirits. Certain sacred rites were reserved to the king or members of his family, thus legitimising the monarch's power. For almost twenty years the Pathet Lao revolutionaries and the representatives of the People's Republic refused to celebrate these rituals, but the population preserved them. Since the beginning of the Nineties representatives of the state have gradually been moving towards these ceremonies again. The development of this significant political process is especially noticeable during the New Year celebrations in Luang Prabang, where the government and the party of the People's Republic now freely participate in and pay their respect to the cultural traditions of the city.

On the last day of the New Year celebrations an exuberant festival takes place where families, groups of friends and work colleagues build stupas out of sand on a large sandbank in front of the Vat Long Khun monastery. The stupas are decorated with rice flour and streamers bearing drawings of the Buddha and the signs of the zodiac. The hundreds of stupas are reminders of the Buddha who has entered nirvana and symbols of spiritual happiness and release. Each grain of sand stands for a burdening thought, an unpleasant memory from the year that has just ended and will soon be washed away by the rising river in the approaching rainy season.

In front of Vat Nong Si Khun Müang the monks have placed
a gilded statue of the Buddha in the double *abhaya mudra*,
the gesture which wards off floods and resolves conflicts.
The lay people of the quarter use a hollow wooden channel
in the shape of a snake to pour lustral water over the statue.
This pure water, which has been blended with frangipani petals,
is then collected in bowls and carried back home for bodily
cleansings that bring good fortune.

On 16 April 1996 a ceremonial procession accompanies the golden statue of the Pra Bang, the palladium of Laos, from the former royal palace to Vat Mai.

Since ancient times it has been the custom for a group of men dressed in black to come down from the mountains surrounding Luang Prabang and walk in front of all the New Year processions. They are the Kha, the original inhabitants of the country, and they come to call upon the rains with the sounds of their bamboo instruments.

In front of Vat Chom Pet on the final day of the New Year celebrations.

The grotto of Tham Ting, the most important Buddhist pilgrimage place in the north of Laos.

The country's ancestors

A wooden house in Vat Aham
On the bank of the Khan river
Near the monks' houses of Vat Xiang Thong Volavihan
April 1996

One of the founding myths of Luang Prabang tells of how, many ages ago, a climbing plant grew so high that it reached the sun, and its leaves cast great shadows on the earth, bringing hunger and cold to the city of Luang Prabang. A kindly man and wife from a higher world hurried by to help the people, and they came down to earth filled with compassion and cut down the climbing plant. During the New Year celebrations these guardians of Luang Prabang's good fortune appear as awe-inspiring masks for a dance in public. They are accompanied by their son in the form of a lion cub. To this day the masks radiate an aura of mystery and sacredness. During the year they reside in a little house at the Vat Aham monastery in two gilded chests that hang, suspended by ropes, above the ground. A keeper, whose office has been passed down for generations within the family, is regarded as a magician who is in constant dialogue with the masks. The dance of the masks, which now takes place again at the New Year celebrations in all the larger monasteries of Luang Prabang, calms the spirits that have lived within the confines of each monastery since time immemorial. In earlier times the dance was also dedicated to the ritual renewal of the kingdom.

The presence of the photographer and the camera at the ritual
that awakens the masks from their sleep once a year, first required
a ritual introduction by the keeper and the ritual presentation
of foods. Only then could the chests be opened, initially to reveal
the robes of the ancestors.

These were followed by the two
deep-red masks of the ancestral couple and the golden mask
of their son. The dancers clothed themselves in the robes
and became Thao Pu Nyoe, Mae Nya Nyoe and the lion cub
Singkham, who they then embodied for seven days.

The country's ancestors procure the water which is ritually poured
over the Pra Bang during the New Year celebrations.
They fetch this water from the spot in the Khan river which is seen
as the dwelling place of the *naga* king, Thao Kham La.

Banphasa: the ordination of a novice

Vat Pak Khan
A house in Ban Khili
January/February 1996

Between the age of twelve and twenty, male adolescents enter one of the monasteries for a limited time. The monks' strict precepts apply only partially to the novices; nevertheless, they too are governed by stringent restrictions. They are not allowed to kill even the smallest living creature, to steal, to have sexual relationships, to lie. Eating and drinking are restricted; they are not allowed to dance, to listen to music, to adorn themselves with flowers, to sleep in a soft bed, to accept money. The young person who submits to these rules and lives in the monastery enjoys special recognition. His parents also treat him with respect and the same restraint that is expected from everyone who visits the monks.

The ordination in the monastery is preceded by a *su-khuan* rite in the novice's home. During this ritual the novice ceremoniously transfers to his mother the merit he is earning by entering the monastery. But the other members of his family also gain religious merit from the young man's deed as it is believed that it will generally improve the conditions of life and, in particular, it will have a positive influence on future life. The transfer of merit to others is of special significance in Lao Buddhism; its distribution is concrete, almost mathematical: half of the merit earned by a novice on entering a monastery benefits him personally, a quarter benefits his mother and the remaining quarter is shared by the father, the people who have donated offerings and the other family members.

In the early morning the hair and eyebrows of the future novice are shaved: he discards his previous appearance and takes his place within the order of the monastic community.

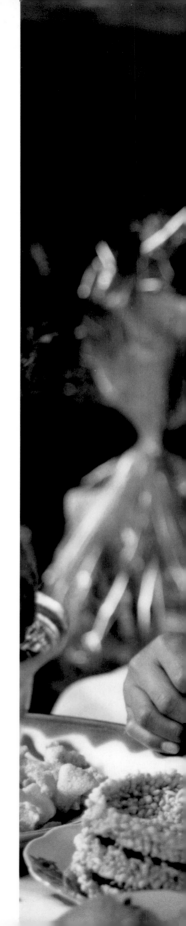

During the *su-khuan* ritual in the house, the novice is clothed
in white material and the gifts for his *khuan* are jointly blessed.
The *mo khuan* reminds him of the circumstances of his birth:
*'Little Nak, you wish to leave the house of the family, you are
moving away from your parents and entering into religion.
You are thinking now of your parents, of their love for you since
they conceived you. When you entered the world, they washed
you, covered you with a big cloth, severed your umbilical cord with
a fine bamboo stick. Your mother embraced you and fed you, she
comforted you when the thunder of the rainy season frightened
you. Now we shall go to the pagoda. All of the necessary gifts are
here, little Nak: the alms bowl, the monk's garments, the offerings
for the monks who will be taking you in...'*

The family takes the novice in a procession to the monastery

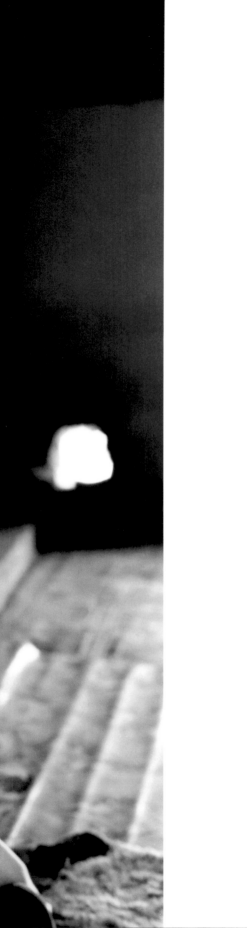

At the end of the ordination ceremony the abbot of Vat Pak Khan
poses together with the novice's parents for a commemorative
photograph. The arrangement of the group illustrates the change
in relationships that has resulted from the ordination.
Nobody's head is allowed to stand higher than that of the abbot;
but the young novice stands on the same step as him. In contrast,
the mother sits on the step on which the father stands; the distance
between her and the monk is the largest among the members
of the small group. Just two hours earlier, during the *su-khuan* rite
in the house, the son naturally stood on the same level between
his mother and grandmother.
One of the guiding principles of the photographic work was always
to wait until the people about to be portrayed had arranged
themselves, and never to interfere in the process of positioning
and space allocation.

After the first alms round
2 February 1996, about seven o'clock in the morning

The festival of boats

On the lower reaches of the Khan river
A sand spit at the entry of the Khan river into the Mekong
August 1994, August 1995

When the waters reach their highest level, Luang Prabang celebrates its festival of boats on the Khan river. The huge dugouts that are launched for the festival are sacred objects because the massive tree from which they were hewn is seen as the dwelling place of a spirit, while the boats are the dwelling place of *khuan*. The boat race is a religious rite which calms and gladdens the *naga* who live in glass palaces on the beds of the rivers. It is the *naga*, mythical beings of Brahmanic and Buddhist origin, half snake and half human, that bring about the rise and fall of the river waters and so ensure that the paddy fields are fertile. The boat race rituals are an example of how other cults coexist with Buddhism in Laos. The two *khuan* who dwell in each boat are called Nang Hüa, and people picture them as young girls. Offerings such as a comb, jewellery, fragrant flowers, sweets and rice wine are brought to them on a tray before the crew of as many as eighty, mostly young, oarsmen is allowed to touch and enter the boat. During the race many of the oarsmen wear the *linga*, a small wooden phallus, as an amulet attached to their belts. The songs they sing while propelling the boats along the river, and especially during training, are full of erotic allusions and directed towards the young women watching them from the bank. Each city quarter participates in the festival race with one or two boats. The individual teams of oarsmen compete, not only with their physical prowess but also with their singing to show which quarter has the most charming girls. Little boats are carefully constructed for the *naga* from the fibrous heart of the banana plant. The oarsmen place them on the water or at points on sand spits along the Mekong and Khan rivers where, according to the legends of Luang Prabang, certain *naga* kings live. These *naga* kings were actively involved in the building of the city and the kingdom of Lan Xang, and now belong to its protectors. This is why one ancient text also refers to Luang Prabang as Sisattanaganahuta, city of the one hundred thousand *naga*; tales create links between the *naga* and the Enlightened One for the benefit of the earth and human beings. One of the stories narrated in Luang Prabang tells of the *bodhisatva*, who appears in the shape of a golden toad king and orders the *naga* to build a road from heaven to earth so that the celestial beings can send the rain to earth along this route at the right time. Before the race the oarsmen lay their oars at the foot of a Buddha statue in front of their monastery, so that they too create a link between the boat festival and Buddhism.

Offerings and rite for the *khuan* that dwell in the boats

Offerings and rite for the *naga* king, Thao Bun Nüa, who lives
at the conjunction of the Khan and Mekong rivers.

Offerings and rite for the spirits of the dead and for a statue of the Buddha

The oarsmen of the boat from the Ban Xiang Thong Volavihan quarter

The boats of the Ban Vat Saen Sukhalam quarter

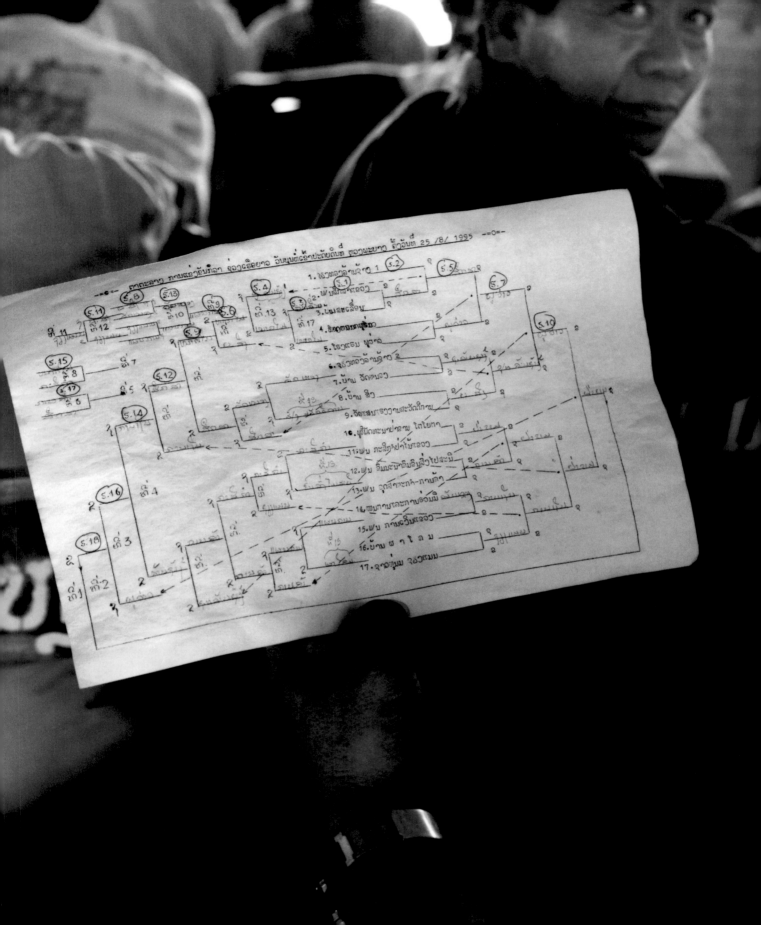

After the race: all of the boats congregate
in front of the Pham Sai pavilion

Healers and magicians

Houses in Ban Khili and Ban That Luang
A monk's room at Vat Xiang Thong Volavihan
December 1997, March 1998

In Laos there are numerous complex commandments (called *kham*), which are activated at difficult moments and in situations of danger as soon as a person becomes ill or becomes involved in an unusual situation. Such taboos instruct a pregnant woman, or a mother shortly after the birth of her child, to avoid certain foods, contacts and activities. A house can become taboo if one of the residents is ill. In this case nobody is allowed to enter or leave it, so as not to endanger the patient's recovery. For every kind of illness there are specialists who perform different rituals to recognise the cause and contribute towards the healing process. For instance, there is the *mo ya* who uses natural medicines, mainly of herbal origin, to heal illnesses that usually have natural causes. The *mo ya* knows the illnesses and their treatments from personal experience or from an apprenticeship to an expert healer. Other, more serious health disorders can be treated by the *mo phon* with a *su-khuan* rite. Illnesses that have been caused by the evil wishes of others are treated by the *mo mon* with magic formulae that only the healer knows. If the illness has been caused by a spirit the *mo phi* is called upon, as she or he is able to enter into contact with spirits. Each of these healers has their own techniques; what they all have in common is that they create a sacred atmosphere for their activities: they light candles, dedicate offerings, recite prayers or formulae and follow a fixed ritual. The majority of healers are women, who traditionally pass on their knowledge and powers to other women. But as the influence of Buddhism increases, this matriarchal transfer of knowledge derived mainly from animistic concepts is declining, and men too can become healers. Successful healing almost always leads to a kind of adoption of the patient by the healer: a spiritual bond has been created, and is subsequently expressed in the social and religious spheres. This relationship is so special that marriage between the healer and the healed is forbidden. Amulets, talismans and magic drawings can prevent illness and ill fortune. The performance of magic actions also cures illnesses, indeed by methods that, if applied in the right way, are infallible. If all of the rules are followed correctly then the magic is certain to be successful because the spirits, like nature, are subject to strict causalities.

Every monk possesses healing and positive powers because of his closeness to the Enlightened One. This is why people also turn to the monks in the event of illness. They are invited into the sick person's home where they recite sacred texts while a white cotton cord unites a statue of the Buddha, the monks and the sick person. The abbot of the Vat Xiang Thong Volavihan monastery accompanies his blessing of holy water for the patient with candles and the recitation of holy texts. The relatives then take the water home and wash the sick person with it.

Healing plants, bones and essences

The magician heals with her hands

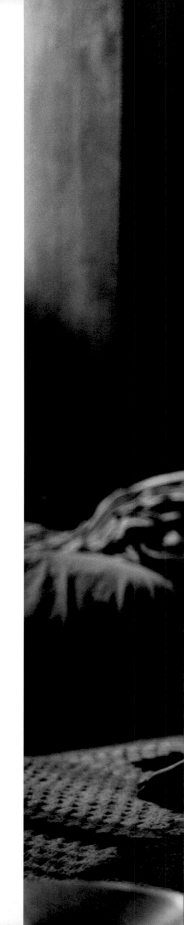

The preparation of holy water in the monastery

Buddhist nuns and meditation places

Vat Pak Khan
Vat Pha Phon Pao
Vat That Luang Laxa Maha Vihan
Vat Phutthabat Tai
October 1995, September 1997

In Lao Buddhism, meditation is a personal, individual effort. It is the fundamental way towards awakening from the dream existence in which every human being is caught, stumbling between the pleasures and pains of impermanence. The meditator is alone with himself and his experiences, and seeks no communication with others, especially not with supernatural beings. In Laos, meditation was always a cultural practice rather than a purely religious one. It is open to everyone, can be practised anywhere and in different degrees of intensity. It is the monks' most important exercise, but many lay people also meditate under the guidance of the monks.

Women can retreat to some of Luang Prabang's bigger monasteries for meditation exercises. They do this either for a limited time during which they observe the eight rules of fasting and abstention, or they live in the monastery for longer, especially if they have no living relatives. In this case they observe a canon of precepts that are even stricter than those of the monks. Present-day Theravada Buddhism has no nunneries, as the tradition of ordaining female novices died out over 1,500 years ago. Until now, recent efforts to reintroduce the *bhikkhuni* ordination have been limited to Sri Lanka and Thailand. This means that in Laos meditation is the only form of spiritual practice open to women within the monasteries. Some abbots in Luang Prabang view these limitations as a contradiction to the equality of all people and genders postulated by the Buddha, who did not recognise the Brahmanic caste system and preached his teachings to men and women alike.

In Luang Prabang the two forms of Lao meditation are practised especially in the Vat Pa Phon Phao monastery and in a grove on the Phu Pasat: *samatha*, the development of equilibrium and concentration, and *vipassana*, the development of inner contemplation and intelligent insight. Precise exercises, behaviour patterns, distance from external stimuli such as colours, sounds, smells or community are the precondition for both these types of meditation. For *samatha* a master names a contemplation theme selected from forty objects. He applies these themes, like prescribing a medicine, depending on the meditator's level of spiritual progress. Intellectual concentration develops step by step; the final goal of this meditation is rebirth in Brahma's world which is considered the best of all worlds. The *vipassana* meditation is designed to promote the insight that all things are transient, full of suffering and impersonal. This meditation is practised while walking, standing, sitting or reclining, either in a wood or in a solitary place beside the river. Its aim is to attain a particular state of contentment which fills the body and the spirit and allows the meditator to perceive all forms of reality. He sees what is truly bad and harmful and extinguishes it; finally, he comprehends the true nature of nirvana.

Meditation cell at Vat Pha Phon Pao

Meditation place at Vat Phutthabat Tai

The fireboats

Ban Mü Na
Ban Xiang Muanne
Vat Xiang Thong Volavihan
Vat That Noi
Vat Phan Luang
Vat Chum Khong Sulinthaham
October 1995

During the rainy season, which lasts about three months, the monks traditionally remain in the monastery. At the end of this period of retreat, Luang Prabang celebrates a Festival of Light where all the monasteries and houses in the city are lit throughout one night with lanterns made of bamboo and paper. In the preceding days, families and other groups of lay people start making bamboo boats and rafts of different sizes. After a ceremony of blessings at Vat Xiang Thong Volavihan in the depth of night the vessels, bearing hundreds of candles, are placed on the Mekong. The current carries the fireboats downstream on a slow, majestic journey. In the middle of the dark river they meet up with other boats from further upstream and continue on their way until they finally catch fire and sink in flames. The spectators watch from the river bank in complete, almost breathless silence. This festival is surrounded by numerous interpretations. Some say that the beautiful boats are sent out in an appeal for forgiveness to the mother of water for what the humans have done to the river over the past year; others see the festival as an offering for the dead who are greeted and bidden farewell with the boats. The gongs and drums of the monasteries are beaten and the full moon shines out into the night. People from nearby villages bring more boats and the children place their own boats with candles and flowers on the river. The monks interpret the rite as a symbol for the renunciation of earthly goods which marks the first step towards overcoming suffering. To them, the steady departure of the boats on the water and their silent sinking into the current of the great river symbolises that moment when the perfect person is free of all ties and enters nirvana.

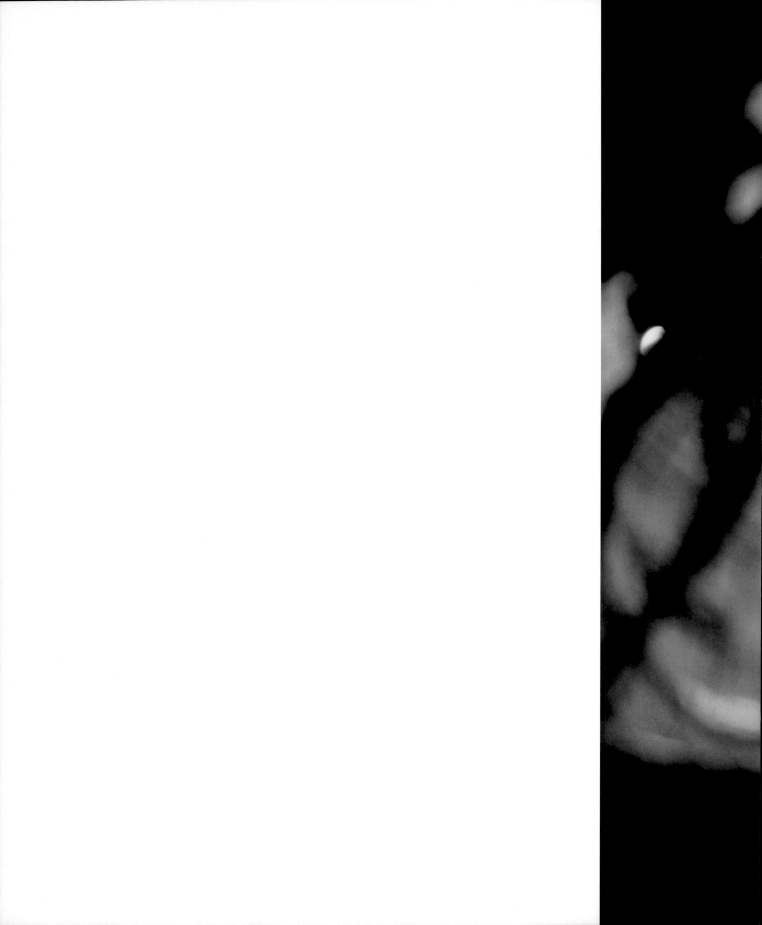

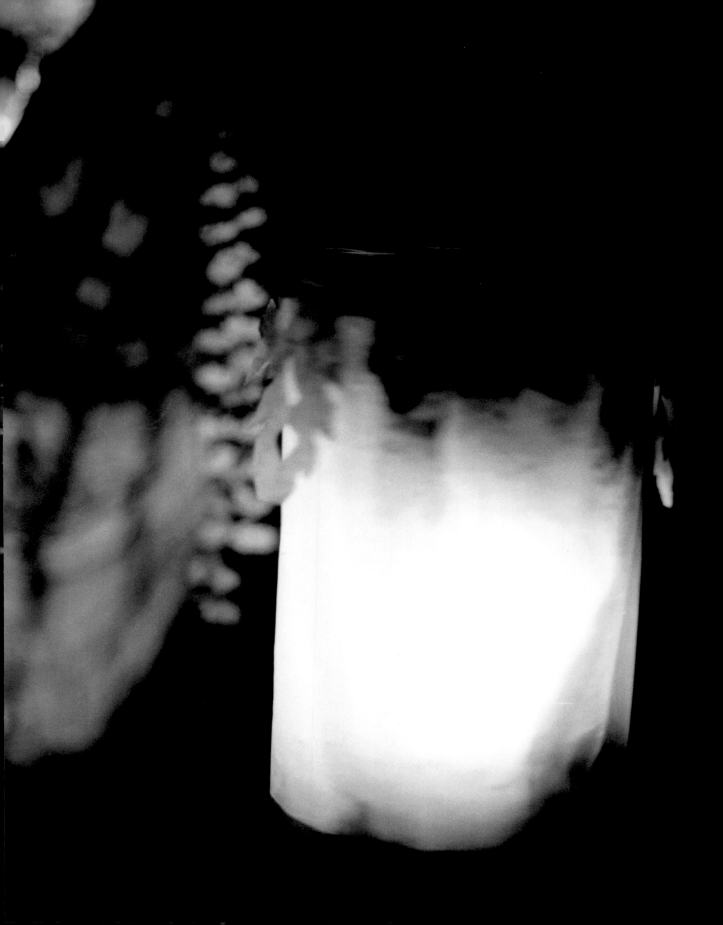

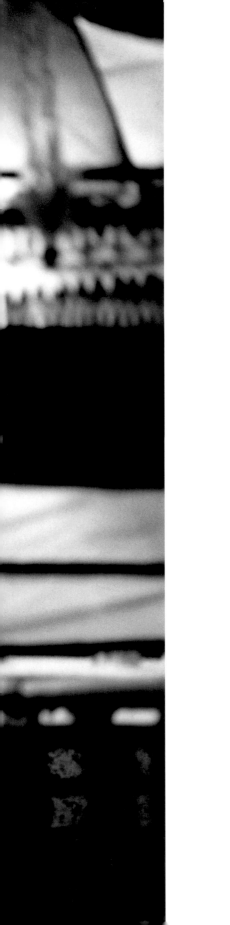

Upasombot: the ordination of monks

Vat Saen Sukhaham
2 October 1995

Monkhood plays a central role in the doctrine and structure of Theravada Buddhism. According to this doctrine only a monk is able to reach nirvana at the end of sustained exercises and great effort in following the exemplary way that the Buddha lived. Nirvana, the extinguishment that signifies the end of the painful cycle of life, death and rebirth. For lay people the monks are mediators between this life and the end of the many rebirths because, through their presence and their acceptance of offerings, they increase the merits that each lay person can gain and consequently give them the opportunity to influence the conditions of future rebirth. Apart from their religious significance as teachers and mediators of the Buddhist doctrine, the monks in Laos also occupy a generally recognised, elevated position in society.

Every male lay person can become a monk and join the monastic community, the *sangha*, for a period of time that he himself determines. During this period he subjects himself to the 227 strict rules that govern all aspects of life and have been valid since the time of the Enlightened One. A new monk is ordained as a member of the monastic community in an *upasombot* ceremony, which is an important festival for the monastery and the surrounding city quarter. This ceremony is the central ritual of Lao Buddhism since it guarantees the continuity of the *sangha*. Certain days that augur well are chosen long before the ordination, and the candidates who have previously lived in the monastery as novices have to prove themselves with an advanced knowledge of the sacred scriptures.

The circumstances of my participation in this ceremony were carefully thought out and specified in great detail. Both the monastery and the day I was to take the photographs were discussed months in advance. The abbot of Vat Saen Sukhaham, Pha Khamchanh Virachitto, acquainted me with the procedures involved in the ordination ceremony and introduced me to the three prospective monks. There were two young men, both from villages in the north of Laos, who had lived for years in the monastery as novices and had just turned twenty (the age for ordination is calculated according to an ancient principle from the moment of conception), and a seventy-five-year-old man who, after leading a normal life as husband and father, had now chosen to leave his family and dedicate the last years of his life to spiritual things. On the actual day of the ordination I was assigned a place in the circle formed by the twenty-one participating monks who were seated on the ground in front of a statue of the Buddha. I mounted the camera on a low tripod, and took all the photographs of the ceremony from this position, almost without moving, and above all without rising to my feet.

On this day the lay people earn themselves great merit with their carefully prepared offerings for the newly ordained monks. The greater the joy with which the present is given and the greater its beauty, then the greater will be the progress and gain for the karma that will affect the future life. This is the concept of the *bun* that is so important in Lao society to this day. It means the good, the beautiful, the right, but also charity, merit, purification. The degree of merit depends little on the concrete act or the material value of the gift through which it is earned. It depends on the level of spiritual progress attained by the beneficiary and the circumstances surrounding the act, and on the beneficiary's proximity to the teachings of the Enlightened One. The women enjoy the exclusive privilege of making the elaborate flower arrangements out of banana leaves and flowers for the ordination of the monks. These arrangements are shaped like a stupa and act as reminders of the Buddha's burial mound, and thus of his entry into nirvana. The giving of these floral offerings to the monks for the ordination is considered an act of the highest meritorious value.

'You have left your house. You know all things of this world are full
of suffering that holds you captive; they are inconstant, unreal,
transitory and oppressive, neither true nor good. You know that
everything is subject to birth, age, death ...'

*'Permit us, venerable teachers, to be ordained as novices
and* bhikkhu *in the law of the Buddha who awakened to knowledge!
Accept us, venerable teachers ...'*

'Venerable teachers, we seek the refuge of the Buddha,
of his teaching, of his community …'

'So hear me: From now on you are members of the sangha ...'

Palm-leaf manuscripts, a teacher and his pupils

The Pha Vet festival

Vat Pak Khan
Vat Don Mai
Vat Nong Si Khun Müang
January 1995, February 1996

Once a year the larger monasteries organise this three-day festival of Buddhist literature where the monks read from the manuscripts of the monastery libraries. The most important story tells of the generous Prince Vessantara (Pha Vet) who is seen as the last incarnation of the Buddha before his rebirth as Prince Siddhartha. A second story tells about the future Buddha, Maitreya, who is filled with compassion and whose coming promises the release of all mankind at the end of time. The festival is a mutually organised event resulting from the complex interplay of monks and lay people. On the eve of the festival, when the monks have completed their alms round, the lay people decorate the ordination hall of the monastery with wild flowers from the nearby forests; at each of the four corners they erect little altars to the spirits of the points of the compass. At the entrance to the hall a richly decorated sermon chair is installed and draped with the most exquisite cloths; hundreds of candles and joss sticks are lit. A canopy is erected to protect the audience from the sun. Beneath the canopy streamers are hung, together with pictures of episodes from the life of the Buddha or Prince Vessantara; a consecrated cord encircles the site. Small trees decorated with bank notes and flowers are given as offerings for the monks. Bamboo and cotton are used to build the prince's horse and the white elephant on which, according to the story, he rode. These are then placed on either side of the Buddha statue.

Monks who are schooled in recitation are invited from the surrounding monasteries to participate. They take turns in reading from the stories handed down on ancient palm-leaf manuscripts, while their large lay audience sits assembled in front of the sermon chair. The chanting of the monks with sometimes dramatic, sometimes lyrical intonations captivates the audience. Many of the audience stay at the monastery for the whole duration of the recitation, about seventeen hours, which is only interrupted for meals and the music of a small orchestra. The *jataka*, the stories read during the Pha Vet festival, belong to the greatest treasures of Lao literature. The members of the audience believe that the texts, insofar as they portray aspects of everyday life, can influence and predict things about their lives in the coming year. The poetic passages are believed to have a beneficial effect on those who listen attentively. As Prince Vessantara was reputed to be extremely generous, which improved his reincarnation, the listeners also wish to show their generosity: they donate money that helps the monks to maintain the monastery and make it more beautiful.

Manuscripts written on paper made from the mulberry tree

Gilded palm-leaf manuscripts

Harvest festival in the country
Ablution of a monk

Vat Ban Phik Noi
Vat Xiang Lak
February 1996

Rice is not only the food on which the wellbeing and health of the community depends, it is also a sacred matter equated with the mythical goddess Nang Phosop. A spirit, the Phi Ta Hek, lives in every paddy field. Numerous legends in Laos tell of the *khuan* that live not only in humans but also in the rice; all of the *khuan* in rice are female beings. To make sure they are favourably disposed, they have to be honoured and called together, so that there is rice in abundance just like at the beginning of time. After a good harvest the villagers take rice to the monasteries where it is placed in pyramid-shaped mounds. The monks then sprinkle the rice with water and encircle the mound with the white cotton cord. In the afternoon the lay people perform the *su-khuan* rite for the rice on the harvested field, without the monks. Throughout the night the young people celebrate with exuberant festivities and in the early morning the oldest monk reads out the myth of Nang Phosop to the attentive congregation of villagers.

The ceremonial ablution (*kong hot*) of a monk is a token of esteem for respected and venerated monks. This rite is a speciality of Lao Buddhism and is not present in other Theravada cultures, although it is known in Mahayana Buddhism in Tibet. The water for the ceremonial washing is carried in silver bowls in a procession to the monastery, where the monk who is to be honoured is accompanied to a specially erected wooden cell. Here he seats himself in his robe on an elephant's tusk. The water that has been brought to the monastery is poured over him through a hollow wooden channel, first by other monks and then by the lay people. During the ablution the monk, who is facing west, meditates on the Triple Jewel (the Buddha, the law and the monastic community). He is then presented with a new robe which he puts on before leaving the cell and proceeding towards the ordination hall of the monastery. While he walks, the lay people spread the finest cloths from their homes beneath his feet and try to touch his robe. This solemn and reverent touching of the robe worn by a monk who has just experienced the ceremonial *kong-hot* washing is a form of meditation that exists only during the moment of touching. After this, readings from the sacred scriptures take place inside the ordination hall. This rite, which often includes the donation of significant offerings, binds the monk to the monastery for at least a year. This means he must remain until at least the end of the next rainy season before he may again make use of the right of every Theravada monk to choose freely the monastery where he wishes to continue his life.

Rites of the night

Vat That Luang
Vat Phon Sa-at
February 1996

At full moon in the third month of the Lao calendar the *khao-chi* celebration commemorates a poor girl's charitable offering to the Enlightened One, while the following night the *makha-busa* celebration is held in honour of the founding of the monastic order by the Enlightened One. The *khao-chi* celebration is a joyous festival where the lay people toast rice cakes over huge bonfires in the grounds of the monasteries. The cakes are attached to long poles that are held over the embers while musicians and dancers perform around the fire. The older generation takes care of the cake-toasting while the younger people court each other until dawn when the time comes to present the cakes, or *khao chi*, to the monks as a food offering. After the monks have eaten, the remaining cakes are freely distributed among all the participants.

The *makha-busa* celebration is the most important religious festival in the cycle of the year. For days the monasteries and all cult objects are cleaned. During the celebration many lay people pledge themselves to the five rules of moral conduct in front of the monks: do not kill any living creature; do not take what is not given; do not indulge in sexual excess; do not lie; avoid intoxicating substances. The central ceremony takes place in the evening. At the big monasteries a great and joyful assembly gathers in front of the most sacred stupa or statue of the Buddha. Holding the triple offerings of flowers, candles and joss sticks in a prayerful gesture, monks and lay people perform the rite of *pradaksina* by circling the stupa or statue three times in a clockwise direction. The first round commemorates the Buddha, the second his teaching, the *dharma*, and the third commemorates the *sangha*, the monastic community. The offerings are then carried to the foot of the stupa and laid there. After this the older lay people follow the monks into the ordination hall where the monks hold the *pattimok* until dawn. This ceremony is devoted to the searching of the conscience and entails the recitation of the 227 rules that govern the life of the monks.

'Tonight we celebrate the great festival of makha-busa, the festival
of the offerings of the third month. In this night of the full moon
our master, the Enlightened One, imparted the rules of the monks,
the pattimok, to his disciples who had assembled to hear him ...'

'The Enlightened One performed four miracles during this night ...'

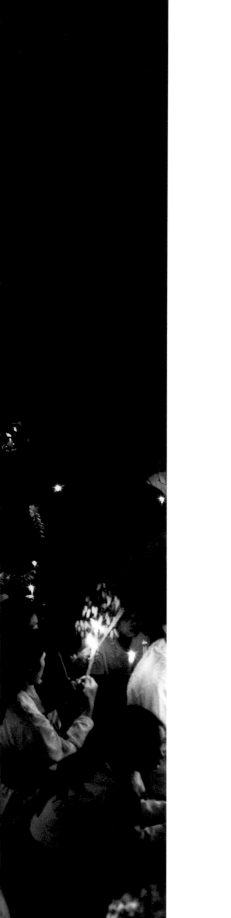

'During this night the Enlightened One himself ordained
all of the 1,250 disciples with the formula *ehi bhikkhu* ...'

The rite for the dead

Vat Mün Na Xomphu Aham
A cremation site near Vat Pa Nya Thüp
September 1995, March 1998

In the scholarly Buddhism of the monasteries there is no definite and final form of life; everything is transient and changeable, in permanent movement like the waves of the sea. This thought is contained in the sacred texts that the monks recite during a cremation ceremony. In contrast to this, many lay people in Laos believe that death is the beginning of a new life: the *khuan* depart from a particular body and will reappear again in a new one or unite with other *khuan*. In this popular conception each death may even hold the prospect of complete salvation, each of the deceased is on the way to final joy. This is why, despite all sorrow, the death of a relative is celebrated as a festive occasion; his or her house is called a 'joyful house' where people celebrate and eat, the monks are invited, and games are even organised for the children. On the day of the cremation the coffin, decorated with gold and silver paper, is taken to the cremation site that lies in a small wood near the town. Here, the funeral pyre is built. Monks recite the prescribed texts. Just before the pyre is lit, the face of the deceased is washed with fresh coconut milk. The photograph of the deceased, which was attached to the coffin on leaving the house, is now removed and the family assembles with it for a commemorative photograph. Only the closest relatives wait until the fire has burnt down completely. They will return very early on the following morning to collect the bones and ashes of the deceased.

When an abbot died his son entered the monastery as a monk
for the duration of the mourning ritual. The family called me to the
monastery to take his portrait in front of the coffin.
Vat Mün Na Xomphu Aham, 30 September 1995

11. Vat Hai Sok (ວັດຫາຍໂສກ)*

/hǎːj/ hai (l.) = to vanish, to disappear; to recover
/sôːk/ sok (l.), śoka (skt.) = sadness, suffering, grief

Founded by Somdet Phachao Anulut in C.S. 1157 (A.D. 1795) in order to ward off sadness and all kinds of dangers from the town.

12. Vat Mae Ka (ວັດແມ່ກາ)*

/mēː kaː/ mae ka (l.) = name of a princess

Founded by Princess Mae Ka in C.S. 800 (A.D. 1438/39). Mae Ka was the foster sister of the treacherous queen Maha Thewi, who was assassinated in that year. The Nithan Khun Bulom says that "Mae Ka came to ask the Sena [i.e. the ministers] to take the queen's body for cremation to her village and built a temple for her ashes called Vat Mae Ka". (Souneth 1996: pp.220-1). Another tradition says that the monastery was founded by Mae Ka, a servant of Princess Lattanaphimpha, in C.S. 1156 (A.D 1794/95). However, at a later time the monastery was renamed by changing the tone of the last syllable *ka* from a low even into a high falling tone. The tone change is reflected in the written form by the adding of tone marker *mai tho*. Thus Vat Mae Ka (ວັດແມ່ກ້າ) means *Monastery of the Mae Ka River*.

13. Vat Sadet (ວັດສະເດັດ)*

/sāː dét/ sadet (l.) = to go (for royalty); title and personal pronoun for princes or royal personages

14. Vat Setthi Luang (ວັດເສດທີ່ຫລວງ)*

/sêːt thǐː/ setthi (l.); seṭṭhi (p.); (śreṣṭhī) (skt.) = wealthy merchant, affluent person, millionaire
/lǔaːŋ/ luang (l.) = main, great, royal

Construction probably at the same time as Vat Xiang Kang (no. 16).

15. Vat Setthi Noi (ວັດເສດທີ່ນ້ອຍ)*

/sêːt thǐː/ setthi (l.); seṭṭhi (p.); (śreṣṭhī) (skt.) = wealthy merchant, affluent person, millionaire
/nɔ̀ːj/ noi (l.) = small

Construction probably at the same time as Vat Xiang Kang (no. 16).

16. Vat Xiang Kang Bolom Vihan (ວັດຊຽງກາງບໍລົມວິຫານ)*

/sía:ŋ/ xiang (l.) = town that is or was the residence of a king; town quarter
/ka:ŋ/ kang (l.) = centre; central, middle
/bɔː lóm/ bolom (l.), parama (skt., p.) = supreme, highest
/wīː hǎːn/ vihan (l.); vihāra (p., skt.) = hall of Buddha's image, place for praying (of laypersons)

Founded by King Sam Saen Thai in C.S. 770 (A.D. 1408/09). The name of the community of Xiang Kang derives from its central position between the two old city quarters of Xiang Dong and Xiang Thong. The monastery has been abandoned and its former ground has merged with Vat Manolom. The famous Pha Bang Buddha image, after being moved from Viang Kham (Vientiane province) to Luang Prabang, was first established in 1489 in that monastery. After two years the image was moved to Vat Manolom nearby. The Pha Bang (Pra Bang) is said to have originated from Sri Lanka

from where it came to Cambodia. The Khmer king gave that golden image portraying Lord Buddha standing with both arms raised forward at the elbows, palms facing outward, to the Lao king Fa Ngum, his son-in-law, in order to promote Buddhism in the newly founded Lao kingdom of Lan Xang. The precious Buddha image, only 50 centimetres tall, was worshipped as a state palladium and should later give the royal capital of Xiang Dong-Xieng Thong its new name under which it is still known: Luang Prabang, "Royal [City] of the Pha Bang". The Pha Bang image was transferred several times during the last centuries reflecting the vagaries of Lao history: Vientiane (1563), Thonburi (1778), Bangkok (1781), Vientiane (1782), Bangkok (1828), and finally back to Luang Prabang (1867).

17. Vat Manolom (ວັດມະໂນລົມ)

/māː nóː lóm/ manolom (l.), (manas) + (āramaṇa) (p., skt.) = mind, heart + temper, emotion

Founded by King La Nam Saen Thai in C.S. 853 (A.D. 1491/92). One account reports that the monastery was built by Sam Saen Thai in 1372. It is said that the Pha Bang image was established in Vat Manolom in 1502 and remained there until 1513 when King Vixun moved the image to Vat Vixunhalat. The *sim* of Vat Manolom underwent reconstruction in 1818, was burned in 1887 and finally rebuilt in 1972. More recently, in 1995, the construction of a wall around the monastery compound was completed. The monastery houses a huge Buddha image that is about six metres high.
The image, whose left arm is missing, is cast in the Sukhothai style of the late fourteenth century. It was placed outside the *sim* until its latest reconstruction. With more than 100 monks and novices Vat Manolom is today the largest monastery in Luang Prabang, and houses the Buddhist primary school.

18. Vat Laxakhü (ວັດລາຂະຄື)*

/láː sā khǖː/ laxakhü (l.), (rāja) + (gṛha) (skt.) = royal, king + house, residence; name of the capital of Maghada (India)

19. Vat Si Non (ວັດສີນົນ)*

/sǐː/ śrī (skt.), sirī (p.) = splendour, glory (honorific prefix)
/nón/ non (l.), nanda (skt., p.) = appreciation, pleasure, delight

20. Vat That Luang Laxa Maha Vihan (ວັດທາດຫລວງລາຊະມະຫາວິຫານ)

/thàːt/ that (l.); dhātu (p., skt.) = bones, relics; stūpa
/lǔaːŋ/ luang (l.) = great, main; royal
/láː sāː/ laxa (l.); rāja (p., skt.) = king
/wīː hǎːn/ vihan (l.); vihāra (p., skt.) = hall of Buddha's image, place for praying (of laypersons)

Founded by King Xai Xetthathilat on Friday, the tenth waxing of the seventh month, C.S. 910. The conversion of the date into the Gregorian calendar gives 27 May 1548 which is a Thursday. In 1900, a hurricane destroyed various buildings of the monastery. The monastery was renovated in 1910 when four new stūpas and a wall surrounding the main stūpa were built.

21. Vat Họ Siang (ອັດຫໍ່ສຽງ)

/hɔ̌:/ họ (l.) = tower, palace, hall
/sǐa:ŋ/ siang (l.) = to risk; oracle

Founded on Wednesday, the third waning of the second month, C.S. 1067. According to Eade's computer programme this date is equivalent to 2 January 1706 which is a Saturday.
The monastery was renovated in 1823/24.

22. Vat Phon Kaeo (ອັດໂພນແກ້ວ)*

/phó:n/ phon (l.) = mount; hill; anthill
/kέ:w/ kaeo (l.) = diamond, glass, precious

23. Vat Nọi Ban Lak (ອັດນ້ອຍບ້ານຫລັກ)*

/nɔ̌:j/ nọi = small
/bà:n/ ban (l.) = village
/lāk/ lak (l.) = stake; principal, base

Founded by a decree of King Photisalalat in C.S. 889 (A.D. 1527/28). In 1899, the compound of the monastery was given to the French post ship company, and the monks took the Buddha images to Wat Phon Xai and Vat Họ Siang. In 1937, the company sold its buildings and the land to Monsieur Doré, a French merchant living in Luang Prabang.

24. Vat Phon Xai Xana Songkham (ອັດໂພນໄຊຊະນະສົງຄາມ)

/phó:n/ phon (l.) = mount; hill; anthill
/sáj/ xai (l.), jaya (skt., p.) = victory, triumph
/sā nā/ xana (l.), jana (skt., p.) = victory; to win
/sŏŋ khá:m/ songkham (l.), saṃgrāma (skt.) = war

Founded by King Anulut in C.S. 1153 (A.D. 1791/92).

25. Vat Si Suvannaphummaham (ອັດສີສຸວັນບະພູມມາຮາມ) [old name] or Vat Mai (ອັດໃໝ່) [new name]

/sǐ:/ śrī (skt.), sirī (p.) = splendour, glory (honorific prefix)
/sú wán nā phú:m/ suvannaphum (l.), (suvaṇṇa) + (bhūma) (p.) = gold, golden + land
/ʔa: há:m/ aham (l.), ārāma (p.) = place given to the Saṅgha for the benefit of the bhikkhus, where they meet and hold discussions about sacred and secular matters; monastery, temple

Founded by King Anulut (r. 1795-1816) in C.S. 1158 (A.D. 1796/97). One of the grand and visually most impressive of Luang Prabang's monasteries, Vat Mai or Vat Si Suvannaphumaham is situated just north of the old royal palace at the foot of the Phu Si mountain. It is the town's royal monastery and is especially known as the home of the Pha Bang image after Vat Vixun was destroyed in 1887 by Họ marauders. During the *Bun Pi Mai* (New Year Festival) the Pha Bang image is displayed at Vat Mai and the laypeople come to sprinkle it with consecrated water. The last vice saṅgharāja before the revolution, Pha Kham Fan, resided in Vat Mai.
The monastery's library houses an important collection of palmleaf manuscripts.

26. Vat Nọi Kang Müang (ອັດນ້ອຍກາງເມືອງ)*

/nɔ̌:j/ nọi = small
/ka:ŋ/ kang (l.) = centre; central, middle
/mɨ́a:ŋ/ müang (l.) = city, town; principality; district (admin.)

27. Vat Chum Khọng Sulinthaham (ອັດຈຸມຄ້ອງສຸລິນຫາຮາມ)

/cu:m khɔ̂:ŋ/ chum khọng (l.) = boss in the centre of a gong
/sú lín/ sulin (l.), sulinda (p.), surindra (skt.) = god Indra
/ʔa: há:m/ aham (l.), ārāma (p.) = place given to the Saṅgha for the benefit of the bhikkhus, where they meet and hold discussions about sacred and secular matters

Founded by Phakhu Kaeo in C.S. 1205 (A.D. 1843/44). Renovation works have been undertaken in 1951 and 1962.

28. Vat Xiang Muan Vajiramaṅgalārāma (ອັດຊຽງມ່ວນວະຊິຣະມັງຄລາຣາມ)

/sía:ŋ/ xiang (l.) = town that was the residence of a king
/mūa:n/ muan (l.) = happy, joyous, harmonious
/vā sī lā/ vajira (p.) = lightning, thunderbolt; diamond
/māŋ khā lā/ maṅgala (p.) = auspicious
/ʔa: hā:m/ ārāma (p.) = place given to the Saṅgha for the benefit of the bhikkhus, where they meet and hold discussions about sacred and secular matters

Founded probably by Phaya Si Sonxai in C.S. 1215 (A.D. 1853/54).

29. Vat Pa Phai (ອັດປ່າໄຜ່)

/pā:/ pa (l.) = forest
/phāj/ phai (l.) = bamboo

Founded in C.S. 1177 (A.D. 1815/16), in a bamboo forest.

30. Vat Kok Pho Thaen (ອັດກົກໂພແທ່ນ)*

/kók/ kok (l.) = origin; trunk or base of a tree
/phó:/ pho (l.), bodhi (p.) = banyan or bodhi tree (*Ficus religiosa*)
/thē̌:n/ thaen (l.) = dais; altar; throne

Date of founding not reported. Situated in the compound of the residence of the former crown prince. In former times convicts were brought to this monastery in the early morning before their execution. There they could receive, for a last time, food from their relatives and friends before being led to execution at another place. The convicts' corpses were cremated at Vat Kok Pho Thaen.

31. Vat Nọng Si Khun Müang (ອັດຫນອງສີຄຸນເມືອງ)

/nɔ̌:ŋ/ nọng (l.) = lake, pond, swamp
/sǐ:/ śrī (skt.), sirī (p.) = splendour, glory (honorific prefix)
/khún/ khun (l.); gūṇa (p.) = beneficent, precious
/mɨ́a:ŋ/ müang (l.) = city, town; principality; district (admin.)

Founded in C.S. 1091 (A.D. 1739/40). A woman is said to have founded the monastery above a lake. The locals believe that this lake was the eye of a nāga and that the Phu Si mountain was its back.
The monastery was famous for a Buddha image of bronze shed in a cloth which remained intact when a fire broke out in 1774. The monastery was reconstructed after another fire, in 1886.

32. Vat Saen Sukhaham (Sukhārāma) (ອັດແສນສຸຂາຮາມ)

/sɛ̌:n/ saen (l.) = 100.000; numerous; very (as a prefix)
/sú khā: há:m/ sukhaham (l.), (sukha) + (ārāma) (skt., p.)
sukha (p., skt.) = health; happiness
ārāma (p.) = place given to the Saṅgha for the benefit of the bhikkhus, where they meet and hold discussions about sacred and secular matters, temple

Founded in C.S. 1080 (A.D. 1718/19). The monastery was repaired several times, the most important restoration work was carried out in

1957 on the occasion of the celebrations of 2,500 years of Buddhism.

33. Vat That Nọi (ວັດທາດນ້ອຍ)* or
Vat Pha Maha That Laxabut Vọlavihan (ວັດພະມະຫາທາດລາຊະບຸດວໍລະວິຫານ)*

/thàːt/ that (l.); dhātu (p., skt.) = bones, relics; stūpa
/nɔ̀ːj/ nọi (l.) = small
/phā/ pha (l.); braḥ (p.) = title indicating respect or worship (preceding certain objects)
/mā hǎː/ mahā (p., skt.) = great, main
/lá: sǎː bút/ laxabut (l.), ⟨rāja⟩ + ⟨putra⟩ (p., skt.) = son + king = king s son
/wɔ́ː lāː/ vọla (l.); vara (p., skt.) = title indicating respect or worship (preceding certain objects), excellent
/wī hǎːn/ vihan (l.); vihāra (p., skt.) = hall of Buddha s image, place for praying (for laypersons)

34. Vat Pha Chao (ວັດພະເຈົ້າ)*

/phā/ pha (l.); braḥ (p.) = title indicating respect or worship (preceding certain objects)
/càw/ chao (l.) = lord, here: Buddha

Date of founding unknown. The monastery is now abandoned. The remains of a 18 sọk (9 m) high Buddha image are now within the monastery walls of Vat Saen Sukhaham.

35. Vat Sop (ວັດສົບ)

/sóp/ sop (l.), śava (skt.) = corpse, dead body

Founded by Thao Thaen Kham in C.S. 842 (A.D. 1480/81). He built a stūpa in honour of his father King Chakkaphat Phaen Phaeo who had died the previous year. The corpse of the dead king was laid out in the grounds of the later monastery for some time. After the cremation his ashes were put into the stūpa and, finally, a monastery was established.

36. Vat Nak (ວັດນາກ)*

/náːk/ nak (l.), nāga (skt., p.) = serpent, dragon; Buddhist novice, candidate for ordination

Founded in C.S. 1130 (A.D. 1768/69). The monastery was built next to Vat Sop. In the sim of Vat Nak also monks and novices from the neighbouring Vat Sop were ordained for some time as people believed that Vat Sop was unsuitable for such purposes because of its connections with death and decay. During French rule Vat Nak was dissolved and merged with Vat Sop.

37. Vat Si Mungkhun (ວັດສິມຸງຄຸນ)*

/sǐː/ śrī (skt.), sirī (p.) = splendour, glory (honorific prefix)
/múŋ khún/ mungkhun (l.); maṅgala (p.) = auspiciousness, auspicious

Founded in C.S. 1125 (A.D. 1763/64).

38. Vat Si Bun Hüang (ວັດສິບຸນເຮືອງ)*

/sǐː/ śrī (skt.), sirī (p.) = splendour, glory (honorific prefix)
/bun/ bun (l.), puññā (p.) = merit, virtue
/hɯ́aːŋ/ (l.) = bright, glorious, prosperous

Founded in C.S. 1120 (A.D. 1758/59).

39. Vat Xiang Thọng Vọlavihan (ວັດຊຽງທອງວໍລະວິຫານ)

/síaːŋ/ xiang (l.) = town that is or was the residence of a king; town quarter
/thɔ́ːŋ/ thọng (l.) = gold; flame-of-the-forest tree (Rhinacanthus nanitus)
/wɔ́ː lāː/ vọla (l.); vara (p., skt.) = title indicating respect or worship (preceding certain objects); excellent
/wī hǎːn/ vihan (l.); vihāra (p., skt.) = hall of Buddha's image, place for praying (for laypersons)

Founded by King Xai Xetthathilat in C.S. 922 (A.D. 1560/61). The monastery, housing at present more than fifty monks and novices, occupies the site at the confluence of the Mekong and the Nam Khan rivers where two nāgas are thought to have their residence. The two shrines dedicated to the two nāgas were preserved at Vat Xiang Thọng until recent times. The monastery also played an important role in royal ceremonies. A stairway leads from the Mekong to the entrance of the monastery, and it was there that important visitors entered the town before being received by the king. Mosaics on the rear of the sim and surrounding buildings depict scenes from Jātaka stories and the famous classical epos Sin Xai. One mosaic also shows the magnificent flame-of-the-forest tree (Rhinacanthus nanitus), called Ton Thọng in Lao, which is believed to have once grown nearby and from where one part of the old name of Luang Prabang, Xiang Dong-Xiang Thọng, derives. In fact, Xiang Thọng comprised the peninsula at the confluence of Mekong and Khan River. Xiang Dong ("Town at the Dong River") is situated in the southern section of present-day Luang Prabang.

40. Vat Pak Khan (ວັດປາກຄານ)

/pâːk/ pak (l.) = mouth
/kháːn/ khan (l.) = name of a river near Luang Prabang

Founded in C.S. 1099 (A.D. 1737/38). Local tradition says that the ground of the monastery was once a place frequented by wealthy merchants from near and far to exchange their goods.
Having become richer and richer, the merchants decided to make merit in order to improve their future existences and financed the construction of a monastery near their trade station. Not unlike many other monasteries, Vat Pak Khan was abandoned several times after the revolutionary takeover of 1975. Between 1978 and 1981 no monks and novices were living in the monastery as the abbot, a member of the Lü ethnic group, had fled to his home place in the Nam U valley. After the abbot's return the monastery was revived for several years but in 1987 it was again abandoned, though only for a short period. Since 1988, Pha One Kèo is the abbot of Vat Pak Khan which has at present two monks and twelve novices.

41. Vat Suvannakhili (ວັດສຸວັນນະຄິລິ)

/sú wánnā/ suvanna (l.), suvaṇṇa (p.) = gold
/khí: líː/ khili (l.), giri (skt., p.) = mountain

Founded by people from Müang Phuan (Chiang/Xiang Khouang) in C.S. 1135 (A.D. 1773/74). The monastery was the seat of the saṅgharāja, the supreme patriarch of Laos, until the revolutionary forces seized power in late 1975.

42. Vat Xiang Ngam (ວັດຊຽງງາມ) or Vat Pa Fang (ວັດປ່າຝາງ)

/síaːŋ/ xiang (l.) = town that is or was the residence of a king; town quarter
/ŋáːm/ ngam (l.) = beautiful

/pāː/ pa (l.) = forest
/fáːŋ/ fang (l.) = sappanwood tree (*Caesalpina sappan L.*)

Founded in C.S. 1161 (A.D. 1799/1800)

43. Vat Pa Khae (ວັດປ່າແຄ) or Vat Si Phutthabat Nüa (ວັດສິພຸດທະບາດເໜືອ)

/pāː/ pa (l.) = forest
/khéː/ (l.) = hardwood tree (*Quercus serrata Thunb.*)
/sǐː/ si (l.), śrī (skt.), siri (p.) = splendour, glory (honorific prefix)
/phūt thā bâːt/ phutthabat (l.); ⟨buddha⟩ + ⟨pāda⟩ (p., skt.) = footprint of the Buddha
/nǔa/ nüa (l.) = North; northern; above

Founded in C.S. 1215 (A.D. 1853/54). According to other sources including Finot (1917: p. 8), the monastery was established earlier at an unknown date but reconstructed during the reign of King Chanthalat (A.D. 1852-1871).

44. Vat Sao Liao (ວັດສາວຫລຽວ)*

/sǎːw/ sao (l.) = young girl
/lĩaːw/ liao (l.) = to look around

45. Vat Chọm Si (ວັດຈອມສີ)*

/cɔːm/ chọm (l.) = top, summit, peak
/sǐː/ śrī (skt.), sirī (p.) = splendour, glory (honorific prefix)

Date of founding unknown. The monastery was located at the foot of the sacred hill, Phu Si, and its stūpa on the top of the hill can be reached by a stairway of 350 steps. Legends tell of the defeat of the powerful nāga who guarded his earthly treasures of golden nuggets from a pit at the bottom of Phu Si and of greedy villagers who tried to steal the nuggets. After both the nāga and the unruly villagers were vanquished, the golden nuggets were used to build the stūpa of Chọm Si. Until the mid-twentieth century, cymbals were housed near the stūpa, and during ceremonial events, the aboriginal Kha were charged with clanging them repeatedly to banish evil spirits that might be present. The stūpa was enlarged in 1796 and renovated in the twentieth century.

46. Vat Pathiap (ວັດປະທຽບ)*

/pá thĩaːp/ pathiap (l.) = royal concubine

Date of founding unknown. The monastery is situated on a terrace of the Phu Si mountain opposite the old Royal Palace. A Bodhi tree from Rangoon was planted here in B.E. 2500 (A.D. 1957) on the occasion of the Buddhist celebrations marking the end of the first half of the religion's life-span of 5,000 years.

47. Vat Pa Huak (ວັດປ່າຮວກ)

/pāː/ pa (l.) = forest
/hùaːk/ huak (l.) = a thornless bamboo (*Thrysostachlys siamensis Gamle.*)

Founded by Phaya Si Mahanam in C.S. 1223 (A.D. 1861/62). According to Finot (1917: p. 8), the monastery was founded already in 1841.

48. Vat Thai Phu (ວັດທ້າຍຜຸ)*

/thàːj/ thai (l.) = end, rear; at the end of

/phúː/ phu (l.) = mountain

Date of founding unknown. The monastery was abandoned long ago. Only a stūpa called That Khao Chi (ທາດເຂົ້າຈີ່) has been left. The monastery was obviously a place where the Bun Khao Chi festival was celebrated with particular effort. Two stone buildings have been constructed in the compound of the monastery. Once used by the royal administrative council (họ sanam luang), today they are the guest-houses for official visitors.

49. Vat Họ Khuang (ວັດຫໍ່ຄວງ)*

/hɔ̌ː/ họ (l.) = tower, palace, hall
/khūaːŋ/ khuang (l.) = sky, heaven

50. Vat That Noeng (ວັດທາດເນີ້ງ)*

/thàːt/ that (l.); dhātu (p., skt.) = bones, relics; stūpa
/nɔ̀ːŋ/ noeng (l.) = to lean; to be slanted, lop-sided

51. Vat Kham Liam (ວັດຄາມລ່ຽມ)*

/khǎːm/ kham (l.) = tamarind
/lĩaːm/ liam (l.) = side, edge, point

52. Vat Pa Maeo (ວັດປ່າແມວ)*

/pāː/ pa (l.) = forest
/méːw/ maeo (l.) = cat

53. Vat Tham Phu Si (ວັດຖ້າຜູສີ) or Vat Tham Thao (ວັດຖ້າເຖົ່າ)

/thâm/ tham (l.) = cave
/phúː/ phu (l.) = mountain
/sǐː/ śrī (skt.), sirī (p.) = splendour, glory (honorific prefix)
/thāw/ thao (l.) = ashes

54. Vat Aphai (Abhaya) (ວັດອະໄພ)

/ʔápháj/ aphai (l.), ⟨a⟩ + ⟨bhaya⟩ (p.) = negative prefix + fear = absence of fear, security; pardon

Founded by King Phothisalalat in C.S. 891 (A.D. 1529/30).

55. Vat Mün Xang (ວັດໝື່ນຊ່າງ)*

/mūːn/ mün (l.) = ten thousand
/sāːŋ/ xang (l.) = craftsman

Founded in C.S. 1170 (A.D. 1808/09) during the reign of King Anulut. In this monastery learned monks educated novices and laypersons as craftsmen such as carpenters, masons, sculptors, painters, artists and potters. These skills were needed to construct and maintain religious buildings.

56. Vat Aham (ວັດອາຮາມ)

/ʔa: háːm/ aham (l.), ārāma (p.) = place given to the Saṅgha for the benefit of the bhikkhus, where they meet and hold discussions about sacred and secular matters; monastery, temple; sim (Luang Prabang)

Founded by King Mangthathulat (r. 1817-1836) in C.S. 1185 (A.D. 1823/24). According to Finot (1917: p. 8), the monastery was founded much earlier at an unknown date but reconstructed in 1818.

The monastery was built at the site where King Fa Ngum had established the shrine for worshipping Pu Nyoe and Nya Nyoe, the two guardian spirits of Luang Prabang.
The monastery is connected with Vat Vixun by an elaborate gateway.

57. Vat Vixunhalat (ວັດວິຊຸນທະລາດ)

/wī sún há là:t/ vixunhalat (l.) = King Vixun

Founded on the second waxing of the third month in the year C.S. 874. This date corresponds to Saturday, 18 January 1513. Vat Vixun is said to have been built on the rice fields of the city's two major tutelary spirits, Pu Nyoe and Nya Nyoe.
The monastery was built with mammoth timbers provided by Luang Prabang's northern tributary states and shipped down the Mekong. Vat Vixun housed the Pha Bang image from 1513 until 1707 when it was carried away to Vientiane. The monastery was destroyed in 1887 by Họ marauders, the sim has been rebuilt in a new form.

58. That Mak Mo (ທາດໝາກໂມ)

/thà:t/ that (l.); dhātu (p., skt.) = bones, relics
/mâ:k mó:/ = water melon

Construction finished on Saturday, the second waxing of the third month, C.S. 876. The corresponding date of the Gregorian calendar is 27 January 1515 which was, however, a Wednesday. The stūpa, the form of which resembles a water melon, was filled with numerous Buddha images many of which the Họ marauders carried away in 1887 when the stūpa was destroyed.

59. Vat Mün Na Xomphu Aham (ວັດໝື່ນນາຊົມພູອາຮາມ)

/mɯ̄:n/ mün (l.) = ten thousand
/ná:/ na (l.) = rice field
/sóm phú:/ xomphu (l.); jaṃbū (p., skt.) = name of a fabulous river from Mount Meru; the human world
/ʼa: ha: m/ aham (l), ārāma (p.) = place given to the Saṅgha for the benefit of the bhikkhus, where they meet and hold discussions about sacred and secular matters

Founded in C.S. 895 (A.D. 1533/34).

60. Vat Pak Huai Mao (ວັດປາກຫ້ວຍມາວ)*

/pâ:k/ pak (l.) = mouth
/hûa:j/ huai (l.) = rivulet, creek
/má:w/ mao (l.) = name of a river

61. Vat Uposot Luang (ວັດອຸໂປສົດຫລວງ)*

/ʼú po: sót/ uposot (l.), uposatha (skt., p.) = ordination hall for the monks
/lŭa:ŋ/ luang (l.) = great, main; royal

Founded in C.S. 889 (A.D. 1527/28).

62. Vat That Fun (ວັດທາດຝຸ່ນ)*

/thà:t/ that (l.); dhātu (p., skt.) = bones, relics
/fūn/ fun (l.) = powder, dust, ashes

63. Vat Uposot Nọi (ວັດອຸໂປສົດນ້ອຍ)*

/ʼú po: sót/ uposot (l.), uposatha (skt., p.) = ordination hall for the monks

/nɔ̀:j/ nọi = small

Founded in C.S. 898 (A.D. 1536/37).

64. Vat Kha Nyang (ວັດຂາຍາງໆ)*

/khǎ:/ kha (l.) = leg
/ñá:ŋ/ nyang (l.) = bird similar to the white heron (Ardeola grayi); hardwood tree (Dipterocarpus alatus Roxb.)

65. Vat Buam Pham (ວັດບວມພາມ)*

/bua:m/ buam (l.) = fertile plain
/phá:m/ pham (l.) = Brahman

66. Vat Pa Nya Thüp (ວັດປ່າຫຍ້າທຶບ)

/pa:/ pa (l.) = forest
/ñâ:/ nya (l.) = grass
/thūp/ thüp (l.) = dense, compact

67. Vat Tao Hai (ວັດເຕົາໄຫ)

/taw/ tao (l.) = oven, kiln, stove
/hǎj/ hai (l.) = jar (for rice, wine, etc.)

68. Vat Müang Nga (ວັດເມືອງງາ)*

/mɯ́a:ŋ/ müang (l.) = city, town; principality; district (admin.)
/ŋá:/ nga (l.) = elephant's tusk, ivory; sesame (Sesamum indicum Linn.)

69. Vat Phon Sang (ວັດໂພນສັງ)

/phó:n/ phon (l.) = mount; hill; anthill
/sǎŋ/ sang (l.), saṅgha (p.) = conch; monk; group of at least four monks who meet in the temple to carry out duties or perform ceremonies

70. Vat Phan Luang (ວັດຜານຫລວງ)*

/phá:n/ phan (l.) = hunter; tray; type of wild areca palm; metal or gilded tray supported on a pedestal
/lŭa:ŋ/ luang (l.) = great, main; royal

71. Vat Phan Luang (ວັດຜັນຫລວງ)

/phán/ phan (l.) = family, lineage
/lŭa:ŋ/ luang (l.) = great, main; royal

The monastery, constructed on the right bank of the Mekong, substituted no. 70 which was demolished by the French in order to build a road. The name of the monastery was slightly changed by shortening the vowel of the middle syllable phan.

72. Vat Phon Phaniat (ວັດໂພນຜະນຽດ)*

/phó:n/ phon (l.) = mount; hill; anthill
/phǎ ñia:t/ phaniat (l.) = trap for catching doves using a decoy bird

73. Vat Pa Kha (ວັດປ່າຄາ)

/pā:/ pa (l.) = forest
/khá:/ kha (l.) = reed

74. Vat Phon Sa-at (ວັດໂພນສະອາດ)

/phó:n/ phon (l.) = mount; hill; anthill
/sá â:t/ sa-at (l.) = clean

75. Vat Phu Dòk Mai (ວັດພູດອກໄມ້)

/phúː/ phu (l.) = mountain, hill
/dɔ̂ːk màj/ dọkmai (l.) = flower

76. Vat Xiang Lek (ວັດຊຽງເຫລັກ)

/síaːŋ/ xiang (l.) = town that is or was the residence of a king; town quarter
/lék/ lek (l.) = iron

77. Vat Xiang Maen (ວັດຊຽງແມນ)

/síaːŋ/ xiang (l.) = town that is or was the residence of a king; town quarter
/méːn/ maen (l.) = angel, god; heaven, paradise; Mount Meru (myth.)

One informant says that *maen* means to "look through" in Luang Prabang dialect. As Vat Xiang Maen is situated between the Yuan villages of Ban Mut and Ban Pak Vaet, Xiang Maen could also be understood as the "city looking through" two neighbouring villages.

78. Vat Chọm Phet (ວັດຈອມເພັດ)

/cɔːm/ chọm (l.) = top, summit, peak; spire
/phēt/ phet (l.); vajira (p.) = lightning, thunderbolt; diamond

The monastery's former name was Vat Chọm Taet (ວັດຈອມແຕດ). *Taet* is a word signifying clitoris. Later on the old name was considered as inappropriate for a religious building and therefore changed to its present name.

79. Vat Lọng Khun (ວັດລ້ອງຄຸນ)

/lɔ̀ːŋ/ lọng (l.) = flatland near rivers; ditch; part, portion
/khún/ khun (l.) = female abdomen; pregnancy (Luang Prabang dialect); *khan* /khán/ in Standard Lao.

The monastery, surrounded by forests, was used for meditation by the kings and the male members of the court of Luang Prabang. Before his coronation, the king meditated here.
A narrow house without windows was used for walking meditation.
As most monasteries on the right bank of the Mekong, Vat Lọng Khun was abandoned after the revolution of 1975 and became a ruin.
It has been beautifully restored by private initiative, using traditional techniques and materials.
The somewhat obscure name of the monastery might be connected to the old name of Vat Chọm Phet.
A legend interprets the two mountains opposite Luang Prabang as two lovers: on the left a young man, on the right a girl leaning against him. Two small hills represent the girl's breasts; Vat Chọm Phet and Vat Lọng Khun lie next to her sex.

80. Vat Tham (ວັດຖ້ຳ)

/thâm/ tham (l.) = cave

There are several caves in the vicinity of Vat Tham, hence its name.
A place for meditation.

81. Vat Hat Siao (ວັດຫາດສ້ຽວ)

/hâːt/ hat (l.) = beach, sandbar; strong current (of a river)
/síaːw/ siao (l.) = a small fraction or portion; to cut across; to touch in passing; kind of jungle tree of the grapefruit family having bitter fruit

82. Vat Phu Phasat (ວັດພູຜາສາດ)

/phúː/ phu (l.) = mountain
/phàː sâːt/ phasat (l.), pāsāda (p.) = palace; home of kings, gods and supernatural beings

The monks of Luang Prabang meditate at certain times near the ruins of the abandoned monastery.

83. Vat Khok Pap (ວັດຄົກປາບ)

/khōk/ kok (l.) = protrusion of a river (Luang Prabang dialect)
/pâːp/ pap (l.) = to subjugate, to repress; to be conscious of pain

Other Buddhist places

84. Dọn Xai Mungkhun (ດອນຊາຍມຸງຄຸນ)

/dɔːn/ dọn (l.) = small island, islet/
/sáːj/ xai (l.) = sand
/múŋ khún/ mungkhun (l.); maṅgala (p.) = auspiciousness; auspicious

85. Họ Pha Bang (ຫໍພະບາງ)

/hɔ̌ː/ họ (l.) = tower, palace, hall
/phāː/ pha (l.); brah (p.) = title indicating respect or worship (preceding certain objects)
/baːŋ/ bang (l.) = thin; here: proper name.

In the period between 1993 and 2000, a splendid shrine was erected for the Pha (Pra) Bang, the state paladium of the kingdom of Lan Xang.

Monasteries situated outside this map

86. Vat Khom Khuang (ວັດໂຄມຂວາງ)

/khóːm/ khom (l.) = lamp, lantern/khŭaːŋ/ khuang (l.) = broad, wide; to impede

87. Vat Ban Xiang Ngoen (ວັດບ້ານຊຽງເງິນ)

/bàːn/ ban (l.) = village
/síaːŋ/ xiang (l.) = town that is or was the residence of a king; town quarter
/ŋɔ́n/ ngoen (l.) = silver

88. Vat Pa Phon Phao (ວັດປ່າໂພນເຜົ່າ)

/pāː/ pa (l.) = forest
/phóːn/ phon (l.) = mount; hill; anthill
/pháw/ phao (l.) = tree, (*Pentacme siamensis Kurz. var. laevis*) (Luang Prabang dialect)

At the monastery next to the "Peace Stūpa" there is the largest community of Buddhist nuns. It is a place of meditation.

89. Vat Ban Phik Nọi (ວັດບ້ານພິກນ້ອຍ)

/bàːn/ ban (l.) = village
/phīk nɔ́ːj/ phik nọi (l.) = hot, spicy pepper

90. Vat Sakaem (ວັດສະແກມ)

/sákɛːm/ sakaem (l.) = etymological origin unclear.

91. Vat Phu Khuai (ວັດພູຄວາຍ)

/phúː/ phu (l.) = mountain
/khwáːj/ khuai (l.) = buffalo

92. Wat Ban Na Xang Voei (ວັດບ້ານນາຊ້າງເຫີຍ)

/bà:n/ ban (l.) = village
/ná:/ na (l.) = rice field
/sà:ŋ/ xang (l.) = elephant
/wɔ̌:j/ voei (k.) = to eat, to consume

93. Vat Ban Pha Nom (ວັດບ້ານຜານົມ)

/bà:n/ ban (l.) = village
/phǎ: nóm/ pha nom (l.) = stalactite

94. Vat Savankhalok (ວັດສະຫວັນຄະໂລກ)

/sá wǎn khā lò:k/ savankhalok (l.), ⟨svarga⟩ + ⟨loka⟩ (skt.) = world of heaven

Founded by King Phothisalat in C.S. 889 (A.D. 1527/28). The monastery near the confluence of the Mekong and the Nam Dong had been of great ritual significance until 1975. Several stone Buddha images and an inscription indicate that the place was occupied by a Mahāyāna Buddhist monastery two centuries before the founding of the Lan Xang Kingdom in 1353. A hailstorm in 1883 severely damaged the buildings. The new *sim* was constructed in 1905.

Abbreviations:

*	abandoned monastery
A.D.	Anno domini (Christian era)
C.S.	cunlasakkalat, cūḷaśakarāja (ancient Burmese era that was also used in other parts of Southeast Asia until the early twentieth century
k.	Khmer
l.	Lao
p.	Pāli
skt.	Sanskrit

References:

Louis Finot, "Recherches sur la littérature laotienne" (*Bulletin de l'Ecole française d'Extrême-Orient*, vol. 17, no. 5, 1917).

Betty Gosling, *Old Luang Prabang* (Kuala Lumpur, etc.: Oxford University Press,1996).

Henri Parmentier, *L'art du Laos* (Paris: Publication de l'Ecole française d'Extrême-Orient, 1954).

Souneth Phothisane, "The Nidān Khun Borom: Annotated Translation and Analysis" (Ph.D. dissertation, University of Queensland, 1996).

Khamman Wongkhotratna (ຄຳໝັ້ນ ວົງໂຄຣັດນະ) ຕຳນານວັດເມືອງຫຼວງພະບາງ [Chronicle of the monasteries of Luang Prabang] (Vientiane, 1964).

Source:

ຄອງວັດພຸດທະທັມ [Monastic Discipline According to the Buddha's Doctrine] (published on the occasion of the cremation ceremony for King Sisavang Vong) Luang Prabang, 1961.

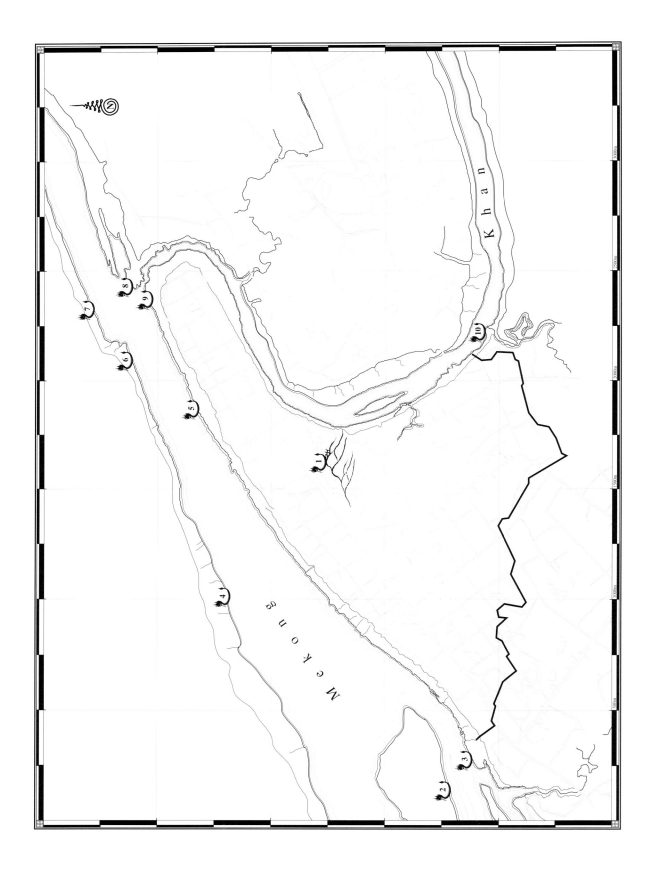

Residences of the Nāga Queens and Kings of Luang Prabang

1 Nāga king (chao)
Si Satta-nak (ສີສັດຕະນາກເຈົ້າ)

2 Nāga queen (nang)
Dam (ນາງດຳ)

3 Nāga king (thao)
Chai Chamnong (ທ້າວໃຈຈໍານົງ)

4 Nāga queen (nang)
Dòn (ນາງດ່ອນ)

5 Nāga queen (nang)
Phom Füa (ນາງຜົມເຜືອ)

6 Nāga king (thao)
Thòng Chan (ທ້າວທອງຈານ)

7 Nāga king (thao)
Kham Piao (ທ້າວຄຳປ່ຽວ)

8 Nāga king (thao)
Bun Nyüa (ທ້າວບຸນເຍືອ)

9 Nāga king (thao)
Tong Kwang (ທ້າວໂຕ່ງກວ້າງ)

10 Nāga king (thao)
Kham La (ທ້າວຄຳຫຼ້າ)

The residences of the nine other Nāga rulers are situated outside the limits of this map.

'... ນາງດຳຢູ່ຄົກທ່ອນ ນາງດ່ອນຢູ່ຄົກເຮືອ ນາງຜົມເຜືອຢູ່ເໜືອທ່າຊ້າງ ທ້າວໂຕ່ງກວ້າງ ອວາງຢູ່ປາກຄານ ທ້າວທອງຈານຢູ່ຜາດຽວ ທ້າວຄຳປ່ຽວຢູ່ຜາເສືອ ທ້າວບຸນເຍືອຢູ່ກ້ອນກ່າຍຟ້າ ທ້າວຄຳຫຼ້າຢູ່ຜາບັ້ງ ທ້າວຄຳປັ່ງຢູ່ພູຊ້າງ ທ້າວບຸນກວ້າງຢູ່ພູຊວງ ທ້າວບຸນຍວງຢູ່ກ້ອນຫມິດແອ່ນ ທ້າວຄຳແທ່ນຢູ່ກ້ອນຜາຊວາ ທ້າວຈົງລວາຢູ່ຜາຍ່າເທົ້າ ອຸດສຸພະນາກເຈົ້າຢູ່ຜ້າຄຳສືບດົງ ທ້າວໃຈຈໍານົງຢູ່ຮັກສາພະບາດ ສີສັດຕະນາກເຈົ້າຢູ່ຜ້າຈອມສີ ກຸງທະນະບຸຣີຢູ່ຜາສຸມເສົ້າ ອຸໂລງຄະເຈົ້າຢູ່ ຜ້າສິບຢ ທ້າວຊົມພູຢູ່ແກ້ງຕ້ອງ. ...'

Translation:

'... The Nāga queen (nang) Dam resides at the Thòn bay, the Nāga queen (nang) Dòn at the Hüa bay and the Nāga queen (nang) Phom Füa above Xang ferry. Nāga king (thao) Tong Kwang guards the mouth of the Khan river, Nāga king (thao) Thòng Chan resides near the Diao cliff, Nāga king (thao) Kham Piao near the Süa cliff, Nāga king (thao) Bun Nyüa on the Kai Fa rock, Nāga king (thao) Kham La near the Bang cliff, Nāga king (thao) Kham Pang on the (Phu) Xang mountain, Nāga king (thao) Bun Kwang on the (Phu) Xuang mountain, Nāga king (thao) Bun Nyuang on the Mit Aen rock, Nāga king (thao) Kham Thaen on the Xua rock, Nāga king (thao) Chong Lua near the Nya Thao cliff.
Nāga king (chao) Utsupha-nak guards the mouth of the Dong river [in the Mekong]. Nāga king (thao) Chai Chamnong guards the Phabat ("The Buddha's Footprint"). Nāga king (chao) Si Satta-nak is on guard on the top of the (Phu) Si mountain. Nāga king Kung Thanabuli resides near the Lum Sao cliff. Nāga king (chao) Ulongkha guards the mouth of the river U, Nāga king (chao) Somphu resides near the Tòng rapids. ...'

Pha One Keo Sitthivong is abbot of Vat Pak Khan in Luang Prabang.
Volker Grabowsky is Professor of South East Asian History at the Westfälische Wilhelms-Universität Münster, Germany. From 1996 to 1999 he taught traditional Lao literature as a DAAD lecturer at the National University of Laos, Vientiane.

Note on the spelling of Lao and Buddhist terms and concepts

In the interest of readability, distinguishing signs indicating the length and sound of a letter have been omitted from the text accompanying the photographs. The terms in question have been set in small italics (*naga*; *bun*), with the exception of proper names, which have been capitalised. Words which have been integrated into the corpus of the English language have been treated in the normal way (nirvana). In contrast, the appendix (maps) uses the correct philological and generally accepted forms of spelling with diacritical marks, so that the etymology of the names of the monasteries and the *naga* can be traced more easily. Although, as in other Theravada cultures, Buddhist concepts in Laos derive from Pali, the text in the book favours the established Sanskrit forms (*dharma* rather than *dhamma*) with which the reader may be better acquainted. In the transcription of Lao terms 'ü' has been used rather than 'ue'.

Thank you:

to the inhabitants of Luang Prabang for their collaboration and hospitality and to

Pha Mao Manivungso, abbot of Vat Xiang Thong Volavihan
Pha Khamchanh Virachitto, abbot of Vat Saen Sukhaham
Pha Bounchanhkeo Photochitto, abbot of Vat Xiang Muan
Pha Khampaeng Khamphilo, abbot of Vat Suvannakhili
Pha One Keo Sitthivong, abbot of Vat Pak Khan
Pha Chanthone Chantiko, abbot of Vat Sop
Dara Viravongs Kanlaya
Dr. Thongkam One Manivone
Prof. Harald Hundius
Ulrich and Julia Dreesen
Mons. Marcello Zago
John Fleming and Hugh Honour
Bernard Faucon
Jean-Claude Larrieu
Nan Goldin
Ursula Schulz-Dornburg
Gigi Giannuzzi
Prof. Gisela Völger
Prof. Giorgio Conti
Prof. Surapon Saenkum
Boonyang Phantavong
Khamsuk Phonesavanh
Birgit Weber
Claude Vincent
Minja Yang
Chitt Chongmankhong
Beate Grzeski
Pascale Rouziès
Joseph Geraci
Karl Brehmer
François Greck
Jean-François Leduc
Prof. Neungreudee Lohapol
Autcharavadee Sudprasert
Gerda Gensberger
Neri Torrigiani
Gleiwit Sastravaha